CW00468730

existentialism
made easy

Nigel Rodgers and
Mel Thompson

pink
(for blondes)

Hodder Education
338 Euston Road, London NW1 3BH.

Hodder Education is an Hachette UK company

First published in UK 2011 by Hodder Education.

This edition published 2011.

Copyright © Nigel Rodgers and Mel Thompson

The moral rights of the authors have been asserted.
Database right Hodder Education (makers).

Typeset by MPS Limited, a Macmillan Company.
Printed in Great Britain by CPI Cox & Wyman, Reading.

Contents

1   Introduction to existentialism   2

2   Living dangerously: the roots of existentialism   10

3   Between birth and death   22

4   Existence precedes essence   34

5   The authentic life   44

6   Freedom, choice and responsibility   54

7   The individual, art and society   64

8   Existentialism and religion   74

9   Authenticity and the absurd: the fiction
    of Sartre and Camus   82

    Postscript   93

1

introduction to existentialism

What is human life about? What does it mean to be an authentic human individual? Am I trapped by the circumstances of my birth, or can I genuinely transcend them? How do I understand and cope with the hopes, fears and anxieties that shape my life? We make choices based on hopes for the future; yet life is finite and we face the inevitability of death. What, if anything, is therefore worthwhile?

These are existential questions. They have long been explored through art, literature and religion, but they are also central to one particular tradition in philosophy – existentialism – which became hugely popular in Europe in the years following the Second World War. The general view of existentialist philosophers is that life is not presented to us already packaged with meaning and purpose, but it is what we make of it.

This chapter gives a brief summary of some key features of existentialism, and points to the continuing relevance of the questions it addressed.

Man is nothing else but what he makes of himself. That is the first principle of existentialism.
Until recently philosophers were attacked only by other philosophers. The public understood nothing of it and cared less. Now, however, they have made philosophy come right down into the market place.

Jean-Paul Sartre *Existentialism and Humanism*

Fundamental, pressing questions – 'What is human life about? Why are we what we are? What does it mean to be an *authentic* individual?' – were ignored by many philosophers in the mid-twentieth century in favour of the analytic clarification of language, the critical evaluation of evidence and similar topics seemingly remote from people's experience of life. To find answers, we had had to turn to literature, art or religion.

Unless, that is, the philosophers concerned were existentialists. Existentialists differed radically from many earlier (and later) thinkers in their concern with the present world. The most famous existentialists – Jean-Paul Sartre, Albert Camus, Simone de Beauvoir – were not academics but writers. They lived and worked in Parisian cafés, arguing, drinking and thinking amid the hubbub of everyday life. This now clichéd image contains a central truth. Existentialists confronted the pressing issues of their age and attempted to find answers drawn from experience, not abstract reason. They looked at the whole of human life, its goals, significance and responsibilities – in other words, what it means to be a human being alive in the world.

Existentialism sees life not as coming ready-programmed by some higher power (God, history, evolution, a divine playwright) with meaning and purpose, but being what we ourselves make of it as individuals. It is a philosophy for the brave, the independently minded. The existentialists themselves were such passionate individualists, frequently disagreeing with each other, that many denied belonging to a movement at all.

Unlike all other creatures (as far as we know) humans are able to ask about the meaning of their lives – not immediately pressing questions about where the next meal is coming from, or how to successfully mate with a suitable partner, but about whether anything in life makes sense. We may be plagued with depression, with doubt. We may pause and not know what to choose. We may be confused, recognizing the freedom to opt for a whole range of different things in life.

Existentialist attitudes are not restricted to the mid-twentieth century. Precursors can be traced back to the very first philosophers, tough-minded ancient Greeks such as Empedocles, Socrates and Diogenes. They too lived, thought and taught philosophy in the dusty streets of their cities, not in academic seclusion. Revealingly, existentialism has given its name to an attitude: 'existential'.

Existentialism conquered Paris with startling suddenness in 1945, the year after the city's liberation from Nazi rule. Artists, writers, actors and students began calling themselves existentialists, although not all of them would have read *Being and Nothingness* (*L'Etre et le Néant*), Jean-Paul Sartre's weighty masterpiece published in 1943. In September 1945 Simone de Beauvoir, Sartre's one-time lover and lifelong collaborator, published her novel *The Blood of Others* (*Le Sang des Autres*), exploring quintessentially existentialist themes of freedom and responsibility. So did her play that opened that summer. In October the first issue of *Les Temps Modernes* ('Modern Times', echoing Charlie Chaplin's film) appeared, with Sartre and his colleague Merleau-Ponty as editors. It became the age's foremost intellectual magazine, gaining a wide readership.

Also that October, Sartre delivered his lecture 'Existentialism is a humanism' ('*L'Existentialisme est un Humanisme*'), attracting such a large audience that some of his listeners fainted in the crush. The first two of his trilogy of novels *The Roads to Freedom* (*Les Chemins de la Liberté*) appeared in 1945. *The Outsider* (*L'Etranger*), a novel, and *The Myth of Sisyphus* (*Le Mythe de Sisyphe*), both written by Albert Camus during the war, also became bestsellers. Although there were other important existentialist thinkers, none quite matched Sartre, de Beauvoir and Camus in combining their three-fold roles as writers, as thinkers and as human beings committed to political action.

For Parisians of the post-war years – hungry, cold, exhausted, horrified by seeing the first films of the Nazi death camps in April 1945 and then learning of the nuclear bombs dropped on Hiroshima and Nagasaki in August – existentialism was no mere affectation. It offered a way of understanding and facing the traumas of the modern world. As de Beauvoir put it, a generation 'had lost their faith in perpetual peace, in eternal progress, in unchanging essences… They had discovered History in its most terrible form. They needed an ideology which would include such revelations… Existentialism, struggling to reconcile history and morality, gave them authority to accept their transitory condition… to face horror and absurdity while still retaining their human dignity, to preserve their individuality' (*Force of Circumstance*, 1965).

Let us, for now, examine just a few of its key features:

Actors, not observers…

Existentialism is a deeply human philosophy. It starts from the point of view that the world is not something 'out there' that we observe and about which we speculate, but that in which we live. That is the defining sense of existentialism – it is about engagement with the world, rather than analysis. Existentialists were concerned to get away from any sense (for which they tended to blame the philosopher Descartes and his claim 'I think, therefore I am') that a person is no more than his or her thoughts. Life is about acting, making choices, using things that come to hand as tools, exploring relationships and the effect they have on you. You cannot understand life by standing back and observing it; you understand it only in engagement.

Essence and existence…

If we were tools, manufactured for particular purposes, we would have our essence predetermined. To use an example that goes right back to Aristotle, a good knife is one that cuts well, because the essence of a knife is cutting. Know the essence of a tool and you know how best to use it. But do I have some predetermined essence? Do I behave as I do because I am a certain sort of person? Or do I shape the sort of person I am by the choices

I make? For existentialists the latter is the case. The famous expression of Sartre 'existence precedes essence' effectively defines existentialism. In human life, essence is shaped by existence, not the other way round.

Living forwards...

We are always planning, looking forward to things. Our mind is filled with the 'not yet' that we want to bring about, and this moment vanishes immediately into a past that is 'no longer'. Yet neither the future nor the past, although they are utterly important to us and define our lives, actually exists in the present except by way of anticipation or memory. To exist means (literally) to 'stand out' – and when it comes to human existence, the key feature is that we are always going out of ourselves, looking for something, planning, organizing the future.

Freedom and responsibility...

Existentialism challenges us to take responsibility for ourselves and for the life we choose to lead. It also insists that we are free, whether we like it or not. We cannot determine the circumstances in which we find ourselves, but we are free (with no opt-out, 'condemned to be free' in Sartre's terms) to decide how we are going to understand and respond to them. I may blame others for the circumstances in which I find myself, but I cannot blame them for the choices I make. I have to take responsibility for my own life.

So exploring existentialism is unlike a study of any other branch of philosophy. It is more of a personal quest and challenge, more immediately related to the arts, to ethics and to questions of personal meaning, direction and significance.

Above all else, existentialism is concerned with the whole of human experience – thinking, feeling, acting, engaging in the world. It is not detached or objective. It does not seek to construct an abstract system to explain everything; indeed, it is suspicious of all such systems. It starts with humankind – from birth to death, a life that is bounded by physical circumstances and constraints, but which also aspires to freedom, to choosing and shaping values, to transcending its present self to become something more in the future, to making sense of a life that is inevitably heading towards death.

Existentialists thought that philosophy should relate to life, to the ordinary concerns and decisions that people face. They rejected the notion of philosophy as a matter of intellectual speculation about the meaning of things in general; for them thought should always be embedded in human experience.

So there was never a single, fixed view of existentialism. That should come as no surprise, for it is curious that existential thinkers should want to coin the term 'existentialism' at all. As we shall see later, Sartre's principal existentialist doctrine is that 'existence precedes essence'. In other words, what you do shapes what you are, not the other way around. Hence it is important to see that there is no hidden essence called 'existentialism' to which thinkers were invited to subscribe. Rather, they approached a common set of questions and areas of interest centred on what it means to be a human being in the world as we know and experience it: the dilemmas of everyday life, the questions of meaning and value and determining what is worth doing.

Do not expect from existentialism a single, coherent system of thought, explaining everything. That is not its style. Think of it as the thoughts of a group of philosophers, writers and artists who, confronted with the tyranny of organized, systematized, scientific and quasi-scientific thought, rebelled in the name of humanity. They sought to explore what it means to be human, how to understand the issues of life, death and personal meaning, what it is to have a past and to anticipate a future, what it means to be committed, or to be concerned, to create and live by values. But it also acknowledges the sense that, alone and frighteningly free in a vast, meaningless world, humankind experiences that profound uncertainty which is given the name 'angst'. Angst starts to appear when we stop our routine obedience to the formulas given to us by society and tradition and start to ask 'What's it all for?'

On from the 1940s?

The existentialists of the 1940s and 50s might have looked a free-living, unconventional, even hedonistic and anti-authoritarian bunch. Some people may have been attracted to existentialism for just those reasons. Yet beneath that there is a seriousness and commitment to create value and meaning in a world from which the old certainties have vanished.

Post-modernism and structuralism in time supplanted existentialism as a fashionable philosophical position. By the 1950s Sartre and others were already seeing it as a limited ideology serving the dominant philosophy of the time – Marxism. But the world continues to pose existential questions, life is as uncertain as ever and science, for all its advances, has not provided answers to fundamental questions about the experience of being human. So the issues with which the existentialists grappled are still with us.

Of course, to appreciate its present relevance, we need to distinguish existential philosophy from the cultural phenomenon of permissive self-affirmation, struggling to say something exciting and positive against a backdrop of desperate hardships and nihilism of post-war Europe. It was the latter which launched existentialism as a fashionable set of ideas with lifestyle attached. The former, as we shall see, has much deeper roots, in questions that were being asked long before Sartre emerged before the crowds in 1945.

Nevertheless, there will always be one character who embodies a line of enquiry more than any other. And in this case it is indeed Sartre – sitting forward across a table, cigarette in hand, expounding his views, in Paris in the years following the Second World War. It was from that particular time and place that existentialism emerged to become a general term for a cultural trend and way of life. Existentialism is what happens when philosophy hits the streets and engages with the questions thrown up by ordinary life.

2

living dangerously: the roots of existentialism

Although existentialism is often identified with thinkers of the mid-twentieth century, existentialist ideas have a long history, not just in philosophy but in literature (for example, Dostoyevsky and Kafka) and in religion. In this chapter we examine three thinkers (two religious; one atheist) who asked profound existential questions and who paved the way for later existentialist thought. They all sought to live out their philosophy, even at great personal cost – examples of Nietzsche's challenge that one should 'live dangerously!'.

Pascal was aware of the terrifying smallness and insignificance of mankind within the universe's infinite space, and of the tendency to try to escape from this awareness into superficiality.

Kierkegaard stressed the personal nature of truth and commitment, rejecting Hegel's systematic philosophy in favour of the example of Socrates, who set out to challenge complacent ignorance in his life as much as his teachings.

Nietzsche, whose atheism and whose claim that it is possible for humankind to find both meaning and direction in life in spite of the absence of God, laid down the challenge for all later existentialist thinkers.

There is but one truly serious philosophical problem and that is suicide. Judging whether life is or is not worth living amounts to answering the fundamental question of philosophy.

Albert Camus *The Myth of Sisyphus* (1942)

Anyone looking to existentialism for the consolations of eternal truths will be disappointed. It does not provide any sort of philosophical comfort blanket. Nor does it offer the quasi-scientific certainties of the logical positivists and other twentieth-century analytical schools. Mathematics and logic, often considered central to philosophy, are ignored by existentialists. They reject the philosophical approach pioneered by René Descartes (1596–1650). Descartes famously declared, '*Cogito ergo sum*', 'I think therefore I am'. By doing so he established the concept of the individual mind that looks at the world like a spectator at a cinema screen or as if through a lens.

This method, if effective at solving some philosophical – and many scientific – problems, has led Western thinking into an impasse from which it has needed repeated rescuing. It ignores the fact that the cogitating spectator is also a human being who is born, suffers and dies. Such 'existential' facts shape the way we experience the world. If the existentialists manage to escape Cartesian sterility, their approach demands the intellectual courage to make hard choices, often going against the flow. Only by exercising this freedom can human beings become fully, *authentically* human. One man in particular (who always rejected the label existentialist) embodied such courage.

In January 1960 the French writer and philosopher Albert Camus was killed in a car crash. In his bags were the manuscript of an unfinished autobiographical novel *The First Man* (*Le Premier Homme,* finally published in 1994) and a copy of Nietzsche's *The Joyful Science* (*Die fröhliche Wissenschaft*). The latter was an apposite book. No one has better celebrated the positive, humanist sides of Nietzsche's thought, often seen as inhuman or nihilistic, than Camus.

Most existentialists followed Camus in *living* what they preached, even when this led to unpopularity or danger. In this they followed another of Nietzsche's rousing precepts: Live dangerously!

This phrase, like many of Nietzsche's all too catchy aphorisms, is frequently misunderstood and taken at its most superficial. Nietzsche in fact propounded a philosophy so radical that it only began to be appreciated well after his mental collapse in 1889. His collapse, whatever its exact physiological cause, seems almost inevitable for a man who likened himself to an intellectual tight-rope walker suspended perilously above the abyss, daring to look down into the depths of human nature. 'It is not the heights but the depths that are terrible!' he warned, foreseeing the potential terrors of a world where God is dead. But Nietzsche was not the sole or first father of existentialism, whose roots stretch further back in Western thought.

Blaise Pascal (1623–62)

'The eternal silence of infinite space terrifies me.' In these words from his *Pensées* ('Thoughts') Pascal voiced the first existential *Angst* (dread, anxiety). A mathematician, scientist and theologian of genius if not a formal philosopher, Pascal was among the few people of his age to appreciate the full significance of the heliocentric system newly revealed by Galileo. In place of the harmonious cosmos revered by pagans and Christians alike, where the music of the celestial spheres leads souls up towards God, Pascal realized that humanity lived on a rock spinning in a silent void. In such a desolate universe, religion could only be a desperate gamble or 'leap of faith', as Kierkegaard later put it.

Nothing Sartre or other existentialists later wrote surpasses Pascal's pessimism about the human condition. 'The natural misfortune of our mortal and feeble state is so wretched that when we consider it closely, nothing can console us,' he wrote. Instead, we try various forms of escapism, either 'diversions' – politics, social life, gambling – or 'habits', such as the routine of the good citizen with his (or her) family and work. Pascal knew what he was talking about. In his late twenties he inherited enough money to live the life of a gentleman, keeping a coach with six horses (a luxury) and socializing in Paris. His contributions to France's intellectual golden age ranged from mathematics, such as his essay on conic sections *Essai pour les Coniques,* to helping prove the existence of the vacuum. In this latter point he contradicted both the ancient philosopher Aristotle, who had written that 'nature abhors a vacuum', and Descartes himself. Beneath his worldly successes, however, religious anxieties were growing.

On the night of 23 November 1654, while recovering from a severe illness, Pascal had a mystical vision. He recorded it on a scrap of paper he later sewed into the lining of his coat and which was only found after his death. 'Fire! Not the God of the philosophers or scholars, but the God of Abraham, Isaac and Jacob!' he wrote. He now rejected rational theology, indeed reason itself, devoting his life to the mystical asceticism of the Jansenists of Port-Royal, which was sharply at odds with mainstream Catholicism. After another near-death experience, fainting away after his coach almost fell into the Seine, he had a negative epiphany. In it he discovered le néant, 'Nothingness', the horrific void beyond life waiting for us all.

At that time newly invented microscopes and telescopes were revealing the universe at its tiniest and its vastest, expanding endlessly outwards and inwards. Pascal realized that humanity is born midway between Nothingness and the Infinite. 'For what is man in nature? Nothing in relation to infinity, all in relation to nothing, a central point between nothing and all, infinitely far from understanding either... He is equally incapable of seeing the nothingness out of which he was drawn and the infinite in which he is engulfed,' he wrote in Pensées.

To many, Pascal was the very first existentialist, three centuries ahead of his true age.

Søren Kierkegaard (1813–55)

Kierkegaard is Denmark's greatest philosopher and a key figure in the genesis of existentialism. He was also a theologian, psychologist, literary critic and rebel who lived his philosophy with self-destroying ascetic passion. Born in Copenhagen, his youth was scarred by the death of his mother and five of his siblings. He was brought up by an intensely religious father, guilt-ridden because he had once cursed God. Kierkegaard inherited his father's melancholy and guilt, once writing: 'Christianity is suffering'. But he also inherited enough money later to live independently. Studying at Copenhagen University, he encountered Hegelianism, the idealist school of philosophy then dominant across northern Europe. (Denmark was still almost an intellectual province of Germany.)

G.W.F. Hegel (1770–1831) had erected a system so overwhelmingly complete that it seemed to his many admirers literally the last word in philosophy. Human destiny or History, Hegel thought, progresses dialectically i.e. by repeated thesis and antithesis, resulting in ever higher syntheses. Finally, History reaches the Absolute, where *Geist* (spirit/mind, a resonant word in German with no real English equivalent) attains full self-awareness. 'History', declared Hegel, 'is the cyclical manifestation of the progressive embodiment of the *Geist*.' For Hegel, here following the mainstream of both Christian and pagan Western thought, the universe is intelligible because it is fundamentally rational. 'The real is the rational and the rational is real,' he wrote. He came to see the authoritarian if efficient Prussian state of his day as currently embodying the Absolute. Hegel also saw philosophy as encompassing religion. He considered all religion as primitively symbolic, despite being ostensibly Christian himself.

Kierkegaard had a mystical experience in 1838 that filled him with 'indescribable joy'. It helped him to reject completely Hegel's grand abstract schema, for it made the individual a mere cog in the machine of historical progress, deprived of all responsibility. He took as his role model Socrates (469–399 BCE), the Greek philosopher noted for his intellectual independence and utter disregard for worldly repute and success – indeed for life, for he was the one Greek thinker executed for his ideas. Kierkegaard wrote his thesis on this founder of the philosophical awkward squad who had *lived*, not just thought, his philosophy.

Socrates had compared himself to a gadfly, stinging fellow Athenians out of their complacent ignorance in his search for an answer to the question: 'How should we live?' Socrates never found an answer to this, claiming only to be a 'midwife' to truth – unlike Hegel, who claimed knowledge of the whole of reality. Central to Socrates' philosophy (notably in *Symposium* and *Phaedrus*) is the analogy between intellectual and erotic passion. The love of truth springs ultimately from the same desire as the love of beauty in an individual.

Kierkegaard's Christian version of Socrates' quest for truth involved similar use of irony, parody and satire. While not fatal, this path made him similarly unpopular, costing him friends such as the writer Hans Christian Andersen, public respect – he was mocked for his odd appearance as well as his heterodox views – and his fiancée Regine. But, as a youthful letter (31 August 1835) reveals, he was determined to seek the truth: 'The thing is to understand myself, to see what God really wishes me to do: the thing is to find a truth which is true for me, to find the idea for which I can live and die...'

Kierkegaard's impassioned Christianity recalls Pascal's in its rejection of easy, comforting, *reasonable* religion. Advocating a 'crucifixion of reason', he attacked the flaccid Danish Lutheranism of his day as strongly as he did Hegelianism. Typical of the complacency he loathed was a funeral address given in 1854 by Hans Martensen, a bishop (and Hegelian), eulogizing another bishop as one of the greatest Christians since the Apostles. Such sanctimonious waffle struck Kierkegaard as intolerable. He saw Christianity not as reiterating church dogma but as requiring from every believer the need to make existential choices that will decide their eternal salvation or damnation. The pressure of such choices creates existential anxiety or dread (*Angst*).

Kierkegaard explored this theme in several short books written under various pseudonyms, some more plausible than others (Johannes de Silentio, Hilarius Bogbinder, Climacus): *Either/Or* and *Fear and Trembling* (both 1843); *The Concept of Anxiety* (1844); *Stages on Life's Way* (1845); and *Sickness Unto Death* (1849). He outlined how the Christian must move from the attitude of the aesthete, who pursues life's pleasures with elegant intelligence but avoids any commitments, via the ethical standpoint of someone who accepts social obligations but ultimately finds life without God worthless, to the religious person, ready to make any sacrifice for God.

The sacrifice Kierkegaard focused on in *Fear and Trembling*, his most vivid book, was that by Abraham, the Jewish patriarch, of his only son Isaac. An ethical hero such as Socrates had to sacrifice his life for the sake of universal ethical laws, but Abraham had to break the most fundamental ethical law to obey an omnipotent God's command. (He did not actually have to sacrifice Isaac, it turned out, as God intervened in the form of an angel who presented a ram instead.) Kierkegaard termed Abraham's act the 'teleological suspension of the ethical'. It transgressed morality to reach a higher end (*telos*) beyond ethics. Yet 'Faith's Knight', as Kierkegaard called Abraham, could not tell at the time he drew his knife whether he really was obeying God. He had to make his choice in a 'leap of faith', a phrase that encapsulates Kierkegaard's whole philosophy.

In *Concluding Unscientific Postscript* (1846) Kierkegaard attacked the idea that faith can ever be the outcome of objective reasoning. Faith leaves no room for debate, for it is the result of an individual's subjective passion, unmediated by church or dogma. Believers must reject any rational support for their faith 'to permit the absurd to stand out in all its clarity, in order that the individual may believe it if he wills it'. Only through faith can individuals discover their authentic selves, and so be judged by God.

'If there were no eternal consciousness in man, if at the bottom of everything there were only a wild ferment, a power that in dark passions produced everything great or inconsequential; if an unfathomable insatiable emptiness lay hid beneath everything, what would life be but despair?' Kierkegaard demanded (*Fear and Trembling*). His ultra-Protestant answer to this question – faith against all odds – had less influence on Christians, reluctant to accept that Christianity is 'infinitely improbable', even *absurd,* than on twentieth-century atheists. Existentialists such as Karl Jaspers and Heidegger in Germany and Sartre in France accepted Kierkegaard's demand that, to live authentically, individuals must reject popular opinion and take control of their destiny by a blind leap beyond reason.

Friedrich Nietzsche (1844–1900)

In January 1889 a retired German professor whose writings were still mostly unknown collapsed in the streets of Turin. He probably had tertiary syphilis. Certainly he had just started an earthquake of unparalleled magnitude in Western philosophy, as he realized. Its after-shocks are still being registered. Friedrich Nietzsche is among the handful of genuinely revolutionary thinkers. He is also among the most quotable and so misquoted. No quotation is more famous than his declaration: 'God is dead!' Often forgotten is the follow-up: 'Now we want the *Übermensch* (Superman) to live!' Nietzsche was an atheist but one of a peculiarly joyful sort. He was also a psychologist of astonishing acuity and a moralist unafraid to face the full consequences of the death of God.

Nietzsche came from a deeply clerical dynasty – his father and *both* his grandfathers had been Lutheran pastors. As a child he played at being a clergyman so often that he was nicknamed 'little pastor'. This gave his adult atheism an explosively personal quality, tantamount to religious conviction, missing in most earlier philosophers. Epicurus (341–270 BCE), for example, had been an atheist but a discreet one. The gods, he said tactfully, exist but live infinitely far from us, unconcerned with humanity. Voltaire (1694–1778), supposedly a deist but really a closet atheist, had had to express his views obliquely in satire, for example when writing about the Lisbon earthquake of 1755 in *Candide*. (This catastrophe had killed tens of thousands of the devout worshipping in church, undermining belief in an omnipotent, benevolent God.) Voltaire's tirades against Christianity were mere squibs compared with Nietzsche's elemental assault, however.

Long study of the pagan Graeco-Roman world had already led Nietzsche to reject his childhood faith by 1865. That year he came across *The World as Will and Representation* (*Die Welt als Wille und Vorstellung*) by Arthur Schopenhauer (1788–1860). Overwhelmed by this 'dismal dynamic genius', as he called the man he always revered as his educator, he adopted Schopenhauer's pessimistic, godless cosmogony. This, roughly following the schema of Immanuel Kant (1724–1804), divided the universe into the *noumenal*, an unknowable, undivided, brutal and amoral 'Will' or reality beyond human consciousness, and the *phenomenal*, the multiple daily world we know. Schopenhauer's bleak view of the phenomenal world as a place of unmitigated suffering led him to advocate asceticism and compassion – qualities notably absent from his own life – to transcend it. Art, especially classical music, could offer a discerning few another escape.

Nietzsche's first great work, *The Birth of Tragedy* (*Die Gerburt der Tragödie*, 1872), shows little trace of pessimism, however. It is a lyrical, intoxicated celebration of Dionysus, Greek god of drama, wine and passion. Nietzsche was the first to realize the irrational god's importance to the Greeks. Like Schopenhauer, he accorded art a central role in human life. 'Only if viewed aesthetically can the world be justified,' he declared, but he was not espousing an escapist art-for-art's-sake stance. 'How much the Greeks must have suffered to be so beautiful!' he continued, realizing that the Greeks' high culture arose from their overcoming their very hard lives. His own elation stemmed partly from his relationship with the composer Richard Wagner (1813–83), another Schopenhauer admirer whose music had fascinated Nietzsche since he had first heard it. 'It thrills every nerve, every fibre in my being,' he wrote in 1868. The two geniuses were mutually inspiring friends until, disgusted by what he saw as the composer's sell-out to the new imperial Germany, Nietzsche became Wagner's most savage critic. Even more significantly, he rejected Schopenhauer's pessimism and 'metaphysics'.

In a succession of books he attacked the deep-rooted metaphysical bias of Western thought, claiming that only this physical phenomenal world is real. In *Human, All Too Human* (*Menschliches, Allzumenschliches*), published in 1878 on the centenary of Voltaire's death and subtitled *A Book for Free Spirits*, he sounded an almost scientific note. With *Daybreak* (*Morgenröte*, 1881) he began his war against Christian morality: 'Christianity has succeeded in making Eros and Aphrodite – great ennobling ideals – into goblins and phantoms… We have to learn to think differently, to feel differently.'

In *The Joyful Science* (*Die fröhliche Wissenschaft*, 1882), he openly proclaimed the death of God:

> **Have you not heard of the madman who lit a lantern in the bright morning, ran to the market-place and cried incessantly: 'I am looking for God! I am looking for God!' This invokes**

mockery from bystanders. 'Have you lost him then?' said one. 'Did he lose his way like a child?' But their laughter dies as the madman pierces them with his glance. 'Where has God gone?' he cried. 'I shall tell you. We have killed him – you and I. We are all his murderers. But how have we done this?... Who gave us the sponge to wipe away the entire horizon? What did we do when we unchained this earth from its sun? Where is it orbiting? Where are we orbiting? Away from all suns?... Aren't we drifting through empty nothing? Has it not grown colder? Is not endless night closing in on us?'

This voices true existentialist *Angst*. We are alone, leading meaningless lives in a godless universe. Pascal and Kierkegaard had also felt such icy winds around them but, while rejecting reason, they had embraced their own versions of Christianity. In his quest for truth, Nietzsche rejected both Christianity and rationalism *without becoming nihilistic*. He thought true nihilists were those who, without a real belief in God, still clung to the ethics of a 'putrefying' deity. In place of this feeble post-Christian ethos, Nietzsche announced the coming of the Übermensch, the Superman, in *Thus Spoke Zarathustra* (*Also Sprach Zarathustra* 1883–5).

'Behold, I am the prophet of the lightning... this lightning is called the Übermensch... All gods are dead. Now we want the Übermensch to live!' By Übermensch Nietzsche meant not a racially superior or genetically modified type but an intellectually, morally and aesthetically higher being. 'What is the ape to humanity? A laughing stock, a painful embarrassment. Just so shall humanity be to the Übermensch... Behold I teach you the Übermensch. The Übermensch is the meaning of the earth.' To counter any undue exuberance this might induce, he propounded the idea of Eternal Recurrence, of everything forever returning. With it came the injunction of *amor fati*, the love of (one's own) fate. The Übermensch must say Yes to life's pains as much as to its joys, again and again and again. Not an easy option.

In *The Genealogy of Morals* (*Zur Genealogie der Moral*, 1887), often thought his subtlest work, Nietzsche intensified his attack on Judaeo-Christianity, claiming that even its highest morals were essentially base. Christianity poses as a religion of love, but this love stems from fear and *ressentiment* (resentment, envy).

According to Nietzsche, ancient aristocrats had called the qualities they naturally valued – bravery, intelligence, nobility, beauty – 'good'. Qualities valued by their slaves – humility, mass solidarity, charity – were simply 'bad'. Judaeo-Christianity, at first a religion of martyrs, slaves and the oppressed, had inverted the old morality. With Christianity's triumph, a 'reversal of values' made slave morality dominant, giving voice to the *ressentiment* of those 'who, powerless in this world, compensate by an imagined revenge in the next'.

The 'incredible revenge' of slaves upon their masters was assisted by Plato and Socrates, who had earlier undermined the heroic values derived from Homer (*c*.750 BCE), first and greatest of Greek poets. 'Christianity is Platonism for the masses,' Nietzsche wrote, meaning that Platonism and Christianity devalued humanity's healthy instincts (and also that the masses cannot do philosophy). Nietzsche called for a counter-reversal of values. This would permit aristocratic free spirits to flourish and humanity again to enjoy life on earth, free from needless guilt about innate sexual and social urges.

Perhaps Nietzsche was half-right. Almost no one can live all the time following the self-sacrificing precepts of Christ's Sermon on the Mount (or the Buddhist equivalent, the *Dhammapada*). We make ourselves neurotically guilty, even ill, trying to do so. Better to acknowledge our real instincts – the instincts of life itself – and plan our morals accordingly. Yet Nietzsche's radical ethical ideas still appear brutal. Schopenhauer, in ousting the deity, had seen no need for revolutionary changes in morality. Nor have many later atheists. Bertrand Russell's renowned atheism hardly affected his liberal ethics – he can sound much like a woolly old liberal. Compared to Nietzsche, Richard Dawkins' loud attacks on Christianity seem merely the spluttering of an irascible Oxford don on television. Nietzsche alone had the vision and courage to realize – and accept – all that the death of God entailed: 'an overturning of the tables of the law'. Although not every existentialist was an atheist, all are Nietzsche's children, forced to re-examine, perhaps reject, every aspect of morality.

3

between birth and death

Many of the key ideas that shape existentialist philosophy are to be found in *Being and Time* by Martin Heidegger. This chapter gives an introduction to some of these, and will also point to the difference between Heidegger's way of looking at what it is to 'be' and the traditional dualist view of Descartes, the first 'modern philosopher'.

According to Heidegger, we find ourselves thrown into life amid circumstances that are not of our own choosing. In seeking to make sense of life, we refer back to our past and also forward to the hopes that we have for the future; we thus live 'in' time, and we live forwards.

The one inescapable fact is that one day we will die; our life is finite. We can usually hope that life can change and reflect our wishes. But in the light of our death we see our life as a whole, and need to make sense of it as it is, not as it might become.

Many of the fundamental ideas and themes that were to shape existentialism appear in Heidegger's *Being and Time* (*Sein und Zeit*). Published in 1927, it was a hugely influential book.

What Heidegger set out to do was to examine the nature of 'being', asking the most general, abstract and fundamental question of all: 'What is it to "be"?' The quest to find an answer to this, which has a long history in philosophy going back at least to Aristotle (384–322 BCE), is generally known as 'ontology'. But where do you start such a quest?

Heidegger realized that the best starting point for a general understanding of 'being' was to consider it from the point of view of the human being; not in an abstract sense, but a person engaged with his or her world living, working, planning and so on. So what he considers is not simply a human individual as might be described by science, 'out there' as an object in the world, but what it is to experience oneself as a human individual, involved at every moment in living in the world.

To do this, he used the term *Dasein*. A literal translation of this would be 'being there' or 'being here'. He is trying to describe what it is to *be* human.

To appreciate a little of this, let us look at just two words, which Heidegger uses in very specific ways:

* **World:** We usually think of the world as the collection of everything that exists 'out there'. Heidegger sees it differently. 'The world' for Heidegger (or rather, 'the world' for Dasein – the human being) is more like a structure or framework within which we live. It is where we find meaning and significance. 'My world' is more than a scientific description of the universe, a world within which I operate. That kind of 'world' is part of me, just as much as I am part of it. My experience of being human is an experience of having a 'world' of that sort.
* **Time:** We usually assume time to be a sequence of instantaneous 'nows', rushing towards us from the future and disappearing into the past. But from the standpoint of Dasein (the human being) in his or her 'world', it means

something quite different. At any one time, we anticipate what will happen next – we plan, we organize, we hope, we fear. Much of what we do, and how we understand ourselves, is given in terms of that which does not yet exist. But at the same time, who we are today has been determined by what happened in the past. We carry with us, if not a burden, then at least a volume of experience. Hence, for us as we are now, experiencing what it is to be human, time shapes what we have become, and what we wish to be. We are who we are, because we live in time. We live by what does not exist – a nothingness – either because it has not yet happened, or because it is already past. This is something that Sartre was later to develop in his book *Being and Nothingness*.

Dasein is thus not simply a 'subject', separable from the 'objective' world outside, but is a combination, a being-with of self and world. *What I am is not separable from the world in which I am.*

Thrownness

We are all born into a set of circumstances, not of our own choosing. We are 'thrown' (not just at birth, but all the time) into our world, which we experience as having this quality of 'thrownness' (*Geworfenheit*). I find myself pitched into it, and within it I have to try to make sense of my life and sort out my possibilities.

The world revealed by science, however, is objective; it is observed 'out there', separate from my subjective experience. It is a matter of space, time, physical entities and forces; it appears to be totally conditioned by physical laws. On the other hand, the world in which the human person finds himself or herself living is more than that. It is not just a world of space and time that could be measured scientifically, but a world of meaning and significance. We move, like a spider, within a web of meanings. Without meaning and direction, without some project, how is one to know what to do, what to choose, what direction to take?

So, if science cannot provide a ready-made sense of meaning, significance or value, we have to set about constructing it for ourselves.

The world in which we find ourselves is one in which we have a particular set of circumstances and therefore a particular set of possibilities. Not everything is open to us – much will depend on our background – but we at least have the freedom to choose which of the possibilities we wish to take.

Goodbye Descartes!

In probably what is the most celebrated conclusion in the history of philosophy, Descartes, determined to reach some point of certainty, realized that (without self-contradiction) he could not doubt the fact of his own thinking. He therefore declared *cogito ergo sum*, 'I think therefore I am'.

And from that famous *cogito* there sprang up the assumption that there was an absolute divide between mind and body – the body physical and extended in space, the mind non-physical. And so, thinking about the way our mind relates to the world, it was assumed that the mind looked out on 'the world' and knew it only through sense perceptions which it processed. That view raised a whole raft of issues. If our minds are non-physical and distinct from our bodies, how can we ever know another person? Do I watch your body, including its actions and its language, and somehow deduce that there is a mind hidden in there somewhere? If mind and body are utterly different, how can my mind produce physical activity just by thinking and choosing to do something? How can my body influence my mind, as when I'm drunk or exhausted?

The mind became (in a caricature of Descartes produced by his twentieth-century critic, Gilbert Ryle) a 'ghost in a machine'. So, from the seventeenth century to the early twentieth, it was assumed that the world was some form of physical mechanism, controlled by its own natural, physical laws, whereas the mind was somehow linked to the body, but never part of the world that we experience.

By contrast, a key feature of existentialism is that the mind makes absolutely no sense if it is removed from its engagement with the world. The mind is involved and active, and that is what gives it character. To use Sartre's famous expression – to which we shall return – 'existence precedes essence'; what we are develops out of what we live.

Cartesian dualism placed a huge gulf between the mental life of individuals and the physical world. The danger of such a dualist approach is that each person becomes an isolated thinking centre. In rejecting this, the existentialists wanted to consider human life as it is lived in the world: a life of relationships, a life that is embedded in a particular set of circumstances, a life that is always aware of the process of ageing and of the certainty of death. For Heidegger, we are thrown into the world, engaged with it, and always living forwards.

Key thought

You can only appreciate existentialism once you see the limitations of what it rejected:

* The attempt to see human beings in terms of pure, disembodied thought
* The assumption that evidence and scientific method could answer all human questions
* The view (summed up in Descartes' 'I think therefore I am') that mind and body are absolutely different from one another, and only contingently linked, and that the self is to be identified with the mind.

And what it made central:

* The human being-in-the-world, making the most of particular circumstances, and trying to make sense of life with its hopes and fears, personal projects and the sense of how very limited human life is, and how inevitable death.

How utterly different and revolutionary Heidegger's thought is here. He is not trying to analyse what might be the 'true' self; he is not attempting to analyse how mind relates to body. He is simply helping us to look at what it is to be a human being in our world. Dasein is how I experience myself in my world; indeed, my world is part of Dasein.

Halfway Husserl

The young Martin Heidegger, while studying in a theological seminary in Freiburg during 1909 and 1910 (he was originally thinking of ordination and studied theology), was fascinated by *Logical Investigations* (*Logische Untersuchungen*) by Edmund Husserl. It was this that led him to switch to philosophy and to leave the seminary.

From Heidegger's perspective his teacher, Husserl, provided a first stage of movement away from Descartes and towards his own position. Husserl's philosophy is described as phenomenology. It explores the world as we experience it. It gets away from the dualism of thinking that experience is separate from reality. What we experience is reality itself.

However, Heidegger was never satisfied with Husserl's work. In focusing on the phenomena of experience, Husserl leaves aside ('brackets out') the question of whether we can know if *what* we experience corresponds to some external thing *that* we experience. In other words, to rather over-simplify the matter, Husserl is still about what happens in the head and sense organs – his phenomena are about *our experience*. And this, for him, was important, because it enabled him to shed metaphysical questions and just concentrate on our own experiences, a process that he felt gave his philosophy a scientific credibility. It was a matter of observation and description, rather than speculation, and that was crucial to the phenomenological approach.

But Heidegger felt that Husserl had not yet properly broken free from the tendency that Descartes had promoted – namely to see the subject self as set apart from the external, objective world. Husserl had come halfway with his phenomenology. In other words, whereas Husserl had seen the necessity of building up the world on the basis of the phenomena that we experience, Heidegger wants to start with the fact that we are in the world, and all our dealings with it are instrumental.

In Heidegger's view, Husserl still saw thinkers as essentially spectators – looking out at the world of phenomena – and as taking an intentional stance towards that world. For Heidegger you need to get away from this external spectator. He wanted to start from an awareness of the self and the world working together as almost a single entity (in other words, where the self is fully integrated into its world).

Heidegger therefore felt that it was his task to set aside the whole philosophical tradition from Aristotle through to Husserl, and to start again. In doing so, however, he inevitably built on what had gone before.

Existentialism logically follows from phenomenology, because we philosophize on what we experience, not on what is 'out there' independent of us. But Husserl could still be understood as having a 'personal theatre' view of experience (i.e. going on inside the head and dubiously related to the world 'out there'). Heidegger shifts away from this. The things we experience are there as the given factual reality of our lives.

Existentialism rejects the 'view from nowhere' idea that science should, in theory, offer information that is not influenced by our own perception (a view which is, of course, challenged by many scientists). In practice, the existentialists sought the very opposite – *the view from where I am*, thrown into life in my particular time and place, challenged to make sense of it. We are always engaged.

There is another way of putting this, expressed succinctly by Maurice Merleau-Ponty in the preface to his *The Phenomenology of Perception* (1945, English translation by Colin Smith, 1962; p. xvi). He says:

> **We must not, therefore, wonder whether we really perceive a world, we must instead say: the world is what we perceive.**

This is central to existentialism. If you start to question whether what we perceive is the 'actual' world, then you start to make a distinction between the world and the perceiving self that leads straight back to Descartes. For existentialism, what the self experiences is its world. The world is where we are and what we do, it is not detachable.

Ready-to-hand

Heidegger believed that human existence (Dasein) only made sense in terms of its engagement with its world. We have already looked at two aspects of this – that we are 'thrown' into life, and that we live forwards. In other words, everything we do in the present moment is informed by our past, and everything aims at our future, expressing our hopes, fears, intentions, plans and so on.

Thus, for example, I can pick up a hammer and use it for hammering (to use one of Heidegger's examples). I use it as a tool to achieve what I want. I have an intention, and the hammer becomes a way of achieving it. But the hammer is not a hammer unless I see and use it as such. Encountering it as a hammer is already to declare my relationship to it – for me it is a tool. We thus encounter things in the world *as tools that we can use to achieve our purpose*; Heidegger describes such things as being ready-to-hand (*zuhanden*).

Now this raises a crucial distinction between his approach and the way in which much philosophy looks at 'the world'. We tend to assume that the primary way in which we can understand the world is through science. In other words, we seek for an objective way to measure and understand what is 'out there' to be examined. We think that science reveals the 'real' world, whereas our own particular points of view represent only a personal interpretation.

But Heidegger is suggesting that our primary way of engaging with the world is not a detached, scientific one at all; it is the engaged one of using things that are ready-to-hand. That's not just a tree, it is potentially the wood I need for crafting something; or perhaps it's a patch of shade I need in the garden; or perhaps it will yield a crop of apples. I am not engaged with the tree in the way that a professional arboriculturist would examine it; for me it is something which has a place in 'my world' because it has significance for me.

In *Being and Time* Heidegger uses the example of a pen that won't work. We examine its parts to see what's wrong. That action is to see it as 'present-to-hand' (i.e. as a 'thing' to be observed) but it only happens because it isn't working. If it worked, we'd see it as 'ready-to-hand' and just get on with writing.

Death

Wittgenstein (1889–1951) famously declared that death is not an event in life. And that, of course, is perfectly true, since we never live to experience our own death. Wittgenstein's statement does no more than reflect the ancient Greek philosophy of Epicurus (341–270 BCE), who saw death as the cessation of experience and therefore nothing to be feared, since without sensation there could be no pain.

But when Heidegger comes to examine death, he means by it something quite different. Death is certain, but its circumstances are unknown to us. It is therefore understandable that many people push the idea of death away – it is something that happens to other people, and that will happen to me one day, but not just yet.

We cannot understand death by seeing the death of others, for that is only a matter of experiencing our loss of them, or their ceasing to be in our world, or of their radical failure to become what they might have become had they lived longer. But we cannot experience what they experience. We can only really appreciate what death means by confronting our own death. Death is what makes you, finally, the person you are. Heidegger's basic question is, therefore: What meaning does my life have in the light of my death?

One thing is clear: in Heidegger's analysis, we always live forwards – our lives are always incomplete, waiting, planning, searching, fearing, hoping for the next thing to happen. The fact is, we never normally see our lives 'as a whole', as something complete. They are always open ended, until... death. And that is where our own death is something quite different from the death of others. If we are bereaved, we mourn a loss. With our own death, our life becomes complete, and to contemplate our own imminent death is to recognize that our life is becoming a whole.

People can all too often try to escape the reality of their lives by trying to conform to some external norm – to do 'what one ought to do'. Heidegger referred to this as *das Man-selbst* (the 'One-self'), and argues that this self always sees death as an *event*, but not something that affects my present life. He suggests that this is an evasion of the real issue.

Being in time

An essential feature of Dasein is that it hopes and fears and plans. In other words, it lives forwards. To be defined entirely by your own past is, according to Heidegger, to think of yourself as a 'thing', a part of the world devoid of authentic human experience. The courage of his writing, and of the existentialism that was inspired by it, was to live forwards – aware of the past but not defined by it.

We shall examine the idea of 'authentic' and 'inauthentic' living in Chapter 5. For now, however, we should just be aware of the basis of living forwards. If you allow every decision to be determined by others, by circumstances, by your own history, then your life is 'inauthentic'. On the other hand, if you accept responsibility for choosing between the possibilities that life offers you, and take ownership of those choices, then you are living in an authentic way.

And this is where Heidegger's insight is so important for existentialism. We live within time, we have a past and a future – neither of which exist in the present moment except as a set of circumstances in which we find ourselves and a set of possibilities in terms of what we are to do. Our life is all about circumstances and possibilities – and that is what makes his ideas about living forwards so important. It is the challenge to own and choose, rather than to remain a victim of the past.

As always, it is Sartre who provides the best illustrations. In *Being and Nothingness* (p. 78) he describes a woman going out on a first date. She is determined not to be aware of the intentions of the man who is clearly chatting her up with some intention in mind. She concentrates only on the literal meaning of the compliments he pays her, ignoring the clear intention that lies behind the paying of such compliments. What the man says in this present moment is given meaning in terms of what he hopes will happen in the future! Meaning is time-related.

And this applies to many ordinary activities. Without a sense of time, we could never read a book. We would read only a single word. Reading a book implies the past (all the words that we have read so far) and the anticipation that we will continue reading. Sartre argued that a consciousness that was only conscious of what *is*, would have to spell out each word. There is nothing in the present moment that corresponds to reading the book.

In *Being and Time*, Heidegger sets out the groundwork for later existentialist philosophy. He sees people as engaged in a world that is shaped into 'my world' of meaning and significance, and which is lived forwards towards death. At every moment, our experience is that of personal meaning, of a past that is given and from which one is shaking free through present choices and concerns, and of a future which is partly given, and partly there to be shaped.

Heidegger suggests that there are three basic structures to Dasein: thrownness, concern and projection. They represent our circumstances, our engagement in the world, and the way in which we plan and hope for the future. This is not the sort of philosophy that Descartes or Hume would have recognized – for they were attempting to set out the logical and evidential basis for making statements about the world – nor is it a philosophy that sits easily with science, since science tends to see its own methodology as the sole means of achieving true statements about the world. But it is a philosophy that maps out the experience of being a human being. It looks at influences, concerns, anxieties, hopes, fears and so on. It is a philosophy that tends to address the most urgent of our questions about ourselves and the choices with which we are faced.

In this sense, existentialism is a philosophy for the streets, one that finds a natural resonance with ordinary people. And here we are back to the heyday of existentialist thought in 1945 Paris – a time of uncertainty but great hope, of people needing to think through what it means to be an engaged human being trying to make sense of one's own personal world.

4

existence precedes essence

In this chapter we examine some key themes in *Being and Nothingness*, Sartre's major work of existentialist philosophy, and the impact of his thought on Paris in 1945.

Central to his work, and to existentialism as a whole, is the idea that existence precedes essence – in other words, that we do not have a fixed nature to which we are obliged to conform, but that we influence *who* we are by what we do. Shaped by our hoped-for future and our given past, we are challenged to accept the anxiety-producing responsibility for our lives.

We are also encouraged to resist the temptation to escape from this challenge by becoming an object – a defined 'thing' (what Sartre calls the world of the 'in-itself'). We should resist any attempt to be defined, particularly by other people, which is why an inability to rectify their view of us can be 'hell'.

There is one idea that is absolutely central to existentialism: *existence precedes essence*. Understand that and everything else follows from it. But to grasp what a radical idea it is, we need to step back and look at the ideas of the ancient Greeks, particularly Aristotle.

For Aristotle, the *essence* of something is what makes it what it is. Know its essence and you know its place in the overall scheme of things, what it is for and what it should do. The essence of a knife is cutting, and a good knife is one that cuts well. To understand anything, it is necessary to explore its essence.

So, on the basis of that older philosophy, the key question was 'What is the nature (or essence) of humankind?' Once you know that, you know how humans relate to the rest of the world; you know how a person should understand his or her own life and its meaning and (if any) purpose. On that basis, you can also ask whether or not humans are free, and how they should act. For traditional philosophy, existence had always followed essence.

On the traditional view of essence preceding existence, the reason you do what you do is because you are made that way. It's your excuse, and you see your life as shaped and determined by your essential nature. It's a scorpion, so it stings; a dog, so it barks – that's the way the world is.

But the claim of existentialism is that, in the case of humankind, this is reversed. Your existence comes first and, by existing and acting, you determine your essence. You can no longer use your essence as your excuse; you take responsibility to shape your own life. That is the central idea and challenge of existentialism, and in this chapter we shall unpack some of its implications.

Although it received its definitive expression by Sartre, the implications of this key feature of existentialism are expressed succinctly by Merleau-Ponty in two sentences from the introduction to his *The Phenomenology of Perception*, published in 1945 (English translation by Colin Smith, 1962; see pp. xvi and xix):

* 'The world is not what I think, but what I live through.'

and

* 'Philosophy is not the reflection of a pre-existing truth, but, like art, the act of bringing truth into being.'

To create one's own truth in the world within which one lives must have seemed attractively empowering, especially since the world was at that time torn apart by the Second World War and its aftermath, and millions of individuals found themselves tossed aside and left to perish. To ask 'What is my truth, and how may I live it?' must have seemed utterly new and empowering.

Like Kierkegaard arguing that truth is subjectivity, or Nietzsche insisting that humankind was no longer tethered to old systems of thought but was challenged to affirm its own future, so Sartre – with his phrase 'existence precedes essence' – expressed the key idea that it was *within the experience of living* that one's real self was to be discovered.

Nothingness

One might imagine that this will be a short section, for what is there to say about nothingness? In fact, as used by Sartre, nothingness plays an absolutely central role in shaping who we are.

Every time I make a choice, I have to envisage that which does not exist. In other words, I have to imagine that I am now the possessor of what I contemplate buying, or married to the person to whom I am about to propose. What I am thinking about at that moment is not what already exists (for the present moment is an ever-diminishing fragment of time between past and future), but of what has been and is no more (the past) and what I might bring about by my choices (the future). But both of these have the character of nothingness – you cannot find the past or the future in terms of some kind of scientific analysis of who I am, since neither exist in the present moment; all you have are memory and anticipation.

In *Being and Nothingness* (p. 33) Sartre gives the example of going into a café where he has an appointment to meet Pierre. As he looks around for him, he negates all the things that appear before him, since they are not what he is looking for. He finally concludes 'Pierre is not here', but that does not mean that he has seen the absence of Pierre in some particular part of the café. The experience of the café becomes 'ground' upon which he seeks the 'figure' of Pierre.

This illustrates the way in which we are constantly searching for that which is not immediately presented to our senses. I go looking for precisely what I do not now see. I hope for what I do not now have. I desire what is not yet mine. Our engagement with the world is shaped by the nothingness which is past and future.

We can look at this in another way. At any one time human beings can turn their attention from what *is*, and consider what *might be*. We are concerned with that which does not at this moment exist – a nothingness that surrounds the existing present moment.

In everything we do, we look to a nothing. I am hungry – I intend something which does not at present exist: my eating a meal. I think of the next word to type on this keyboard; at the moment of thinking it, it does not yet exist. We are always aiming at that which we are not, at the 'nothing' which is future, while influenced by our own personal history, the 'nothing' which is past. If we were only aware of the present, life would be (literally) hopeless.

Angst

Kierkegaard described Angst as 'the dizziness of freedom', it is what happens when the familiar is removed and one is confronted with one's own freedom. It is a non-specific sense of anxiety, a feeling of being way out of one's depth and in deep, threatening water; it is the moment of leaving home, of facing the unknown.

Angst is not the same as fear. Fear is directed towards some object – if we are frightened, we are frightened of something, some person, object or event that we want to avoid. Angst is different, in that it is a general sense of being anxious, of feeling not-at-home in the world, of things generally not being right.

Angst is best illustrated by considering the way in which people escape from it. Heidegger (in *Being and Time*) suggests that they do so by hiding and trying to lose themselves in the world – what he calls 'falling'. It is a common phenomenon. People throw themselves into work, or a hobby, or a relationship, or some hopeless ambition. They seek to make success in that limited field a reason for living. Take away their work, or their family, or their status, and they feel utterly diminished, lost, uncertain about who they are anymore.

Angst is also experienced as we face the prospect of our own death – for that is the point at which one's being is exposed, no longer able to hide in some external source of comfort. Angst is what Heidegger called 'being-towards-death'. It is not dying that is the cause of Angst, but the fact that life is finite. We encounter Angst the moment we stand back and attempt to get an objective look at ourselves. We see our own finitude and the meaninglessness of the world around us.

Angst is the experience of the 'nothing', it is the sense that the world is slipping away from us. Angst also requires reflection. Fear can be an immediate, unreflecting response to an impending threat. But Angst is something more than that, it arises when we reflect on our situation (I may be ruined by this; I may be killed or wounded). To take Sartre's example (from *Being and Nothingness*, pp. 54–5), if I walk along a narrow path beside a precipice I fear falling off the edge, but may take steps to alleviate that fear by paying attention to where I put my feet. But I may also sense that these steps of mine may not be enough to prevent my falling. It is this that produces anguish (Angst) since I find myself in jeopardy.

Within existential thought, Angst is related very closely to nothingness and to freedom. It is also the result of dispensing with a life dominated by 'doing the right thing' in terms of social expectations. Sartre referred to rules, signs, tax forms, policemen, as 'guard rails' against anguish. In other words, we use them to keep us from looking over and falling into an abyss of personal uncertainty. But for the person who contemplates his or her own freedom, all the guard rails collapse. In a conclusion that has implications for morality, Sartre says:

> *I emerge alone and in anguish confronting the unique and original project which constitutes my being... I have to realize the meaning of the world and of my essence; I make my decision concerning them – without justification and without excuse.*

And he concludes:

> *Anguish then is the reflective apprehension of freedom by itself.*

Being and Nothingness, p. 63

The 'in-itself' and the 'for-itself'

Sartre's distinction between the 'in-itself' and the 'for-itself' is absolutely fundamental to his philosophy, because it represents two very different ways of existing in the world.

A non-conscious object exists 'in-itself': it is what it is and nothing more. The world of the 'in-itself' may be examined by science; it is the world of things.

To relate to the world as a human being, to be conscious and engaged, is to exist as 'for-itself'.

A human being is always aware of a lack, of striving to be something more, of wanting to achieve a completeness that it does not yet possess. 'Human reality is, before all, its own nothingness' (*Being and Nothingness*, p. 112). If I consider only a thing (something in the world of the in-itself) then it is exactly what it is at this moment. It has a fixed self. But consciousness, the 'for-itself', is always aware of something more. To use Sartre's wonderful image, 'It is the full moon that confers on the crescent moon its being as crescent; what-is-not determines what-is' (*Being and Nothingness*, p. 111).

But – and this is the key to the whole existentialist approach to authentic living, freedom and responsibility – there is always a temptation for the 'for-itself' to want to define itself in terms of an 'in-itself'. To put it crudely: for consciousness to become a 'thing'. In other words, there is a human craving to understand oneself as a totality, as a defined and known entity. But this cannot happen, for as soon as it tries to be fixed and defined, the 'for-itself' vanishes. Hence, there is constant frustration, wanting to know ourselves in a way that is impossible.

We live forwards, we include in ourselves the 'nothing' that is all we are not at the moment. Our past is the in-itself that we were at that time but, of course, because we are still alive, that past in-itself is already being surpassed. It would be so tempting to see our whole life as a single 'thing' to which we could point and say 'Yes, that is absolutely me!' but it cannot happen. We are forced to be free, to choose what we will do, and to change ourselves in doing so.

Hell is other people

This, probably Sartre's best-known quote, comes at the end of his play *No Exit* (*Huis Clos*), where the characters find themselves in hell, and realize that they need no further torture than what they are able to do to one another. But it reflects a key feature of part III of *Being and Nothingness*: the idea of 'being-for-others' – in other words, what I am as observed by other people.

We can treat people as objects, as performing a service for us, for example. But there are other occasions when we are aware that the other person is clearly in a position to take a view of us, and that we might become as much an object for them as they can be for us. Sartre illustrates this (p. 283) with an account of someone with his ear glued to a door, trying to overhear the conversation within, and then peeping through the keyhole. In the moment he does that, he is not conscious of himself, but totally engrossed in what is happening inside the room. Then, suddenly he becomes aware of someone behind him; he himself is being observed.

At that moment, Sartre observes, my sense of myself changes because I am also aware of being scrutinized and judged by another person. I am no longer simply interested in what is happening beyond that door, I have become a 'peeping Tom'. Nothing else but another human being can give me that sense of personal embarrassment, shame or whatever.

That is a rather extreme example of a general situation, namely that we are always encountering and being encountered by other people. They take a view of us, see us as an 'object' within their world. Far from being a free 'for-itself' engaged in our world, we find that we are limited by the gaze of others; we suddenly become aware of ourselves in the mode of in-itself, as a thing. In the case of the 'peeping Tom', instead of simply observing, he now becomes exactly a 'peeping Tom', he is characterized. His self is narrowed into the in-itself world of objects (in this case, an object called a 'peeping Tom').

As other people see me, I become an object for them. And I react emotionally to myself as seen by others – by feeling shame, for example – and accept their objective observation, their value judgements.

At death, the for-itself turns into an in-itself. In other words, it becomes something to be remembered, fixed and part of the past that people remember. It is no longer the forward living being that it was while alive. In *Being and Nothingness* (p. 138) Sartre says 'at the moment of death the chips are down, there remains not a card to play... At the moment of death we *are*; that is, we are defenceless before the judgements of others.'

What makes it so hard to think of oneself dead, according to Sartre, is that – until the point of your death – you can always assume that you can change, that whatever view other people have of you, it is always possible that they are wrong, and that you can be better than they thought, or different in some way. But from the perspective of death, change is no longer an option. You are, in the eyes of those who knew you, fixed for all time. There is nothing you can do now to change their opinion. That is why 'hell is other people' – not just that they are awful to live with, but that they are able to look at you and pass judgement. You are stuck with who you have been, rather than what you might hope to become.

Or, to put it in Sartre's philosophical terminology: 'By death, the for-itself has changed forever into an in-itself in that it has slipped entirely into the past' (*Being and Nothingness*, p. 138).

Taking Paris by storm!

On 29 October 1945, Sartre gave a lecture entitled 'Existentialism is a Humanism'. Far from being a quiet and restrained affair, the crowds flocked in, clearly anticipating that this was going to be no ordinary philosophy lecture.

Aware that people regarded existentialism as something new and scandalous, he purported to explain that 'this is of all teachings the least scandalous and the most austere: it is intended strictly for technicians and philosophers'. But one wonders whether that was not simply a device for hyping up the anticipation of his audience, for he wanted to present his philosophy as one that was alarming because, above all, it 'confronts man with a possibility of choice' (page 2 of *Existentialism and Humanism*, the book that contains the lecture and some responses to it).

Sartre returned time and again to this challenge – that we are forced to choose what we will do, and that 'you are nothing else but what you live' and that 'this theory alone is compatible with the dignity of man, it is the only one that does not make man into an object' (*Existentialism and Humanism*, p. 52).

And his language was clearly intended to engage his audience, rather than explore the subject in a detached, philosophical way: 'Life is nothing until it is lived; but it is yours to make sense of, and the value of it is nothing else but the sense that you choose.'

And his final fling was to argue that, even if God were to exist (which, of course, he believed he did not) that would make no difference to the challenge to give one's life direction.

Whatever the shortcomings of that particular lecture, it was *the* event for existentialism, the symbol that a new philosophy had arrived that would challenge people to take responsibility for their lives. People started calling themselves existentialists even if they knew relatively little about Sartre's philosophy.

5

the authentic life

Existentialism is concerned with how we, as human beings, understand and respond to life, as opposed to a detached, objective, scientific view of existence. Central to this personal engagement with life is the idea that we should live an 'authentic' life, taking responsibility for our own decisions and affirming ourselves as individuals.

The alternative is to allow ourselves to be determined by circumstances, to accept a particular role in life and act it out, rather than being true to our own individuality; it is to settle for living as a 'thing' rather than as a human being.

In this chapter we shall look at self-affirmation and the recognition that one is more than the limited roles or masks that one might adopt for an easy and predictable life, noting especially the implication this has for women, and finally at the way in which authenticity requires courage in a world that is often unreasonable.

Man is nothing else but what he makes of himself.

Sartre's 'Existentialism is a Humanism'

The reason for embracing existential questions was set out by Karl Jaspers in the opening of his *Philosophy*, published in 1932, in a chapter headed 'Philosophy starts with our situation', and it may serve to recap where we have come so far in our study of existentialism.

I do not begin at the beginning when I ask questions such as 'What is being?' or 'Why is anything at all? Why not nothing?' or 'Who am I?' or 'What do I really want?' These questions arise from a situation in which, coming from a past, I find myself.

(English translation E.B. Ashton, University of Chicago Press, 1969)

In other words, philosophy starts when I find myself in a world in which I need to take bearings. I look for answers that will give me support.

* It is concerned with engaged human living, how we understand and respond to life, rather than a detached or scientific view of existence.
* It is concerned with consciousness, which is what distinguishes us from 'things'.
* Consciousness is always directed towards something – it is 'consciousness of'. It is not itself a 'thing'.
* Hence the danger of allowing ourselves to become 'things' rather than persons – to slip back into the world of the 'in-itself' rather than the 'for-itself'.
* To live the authentic life is to avoid this danger of becoming a 'thing'.

These last two points lead us to ask what authentic living means and how it is possible.

In some sense, a concern with authentic living has always been a feature of philosophy since the time of Plato, but it was given particular emphasis by Kierkegaard who, in his book *Either/Or* (*Enten/Eller*), describes three stages of life:

1 The aesthetic: superficially concerned with the senses.
2 The ethical: living in obedience to accepted moral standards.

3 The religious: moving beyond conventional morality into the realm of personal conviction, risk and anxiety.

Moving into the third of these stages involves living without any external guarantees of security – it is striving to be yourself, without retreating into mere convention, or the superficial life of physical pleasure.

Heidegger speaks about authentic and inauthentic modes of living – a distinction taken up by Sartre in his discussion of what he calls 'bad faith', and exemplified by many of the feminist arguments put forward by Simone de Beauvoir.

So how is authentic life achieved?

Heidegger claimed, in *Being and Time*, that to exist authentically is to choose the possibilities of my existence. In other words, it is to be myself, and take responsibility for being myself, by selecting from the possibilities that life provides (in the situation into which I have been thrown). The opposite of this authentic existence is to do what 'one' does, to follow 'das Man' – in other words, to accept what is generally thought of as the correct thing, to accept the norms of society in an unquestioning way, falling back into what Kierkegaard called the 'ethical stage'. It is to refuse to take responsibility for your own free choices.

Affirming oneself

Nietzsche saw a dying of the old certainties, expressed in his language about the Death of God (in *The Joyful Science*, 1882). The world had become colder, less predictable, less comfortable. And in the face of that, his challenge was to create and affirm the Übermensch, the Superman, not as a fact, but as a choice. His works have been hugely influential, and not just for existentialists, in that they emphasize the challenge of human self-affirmation in a world where values and direction are not guaranteed, but have to be created – see particularly his *Thus Spoke Zarathustra* (1883–5) and *Beyond Good and Evil* (1886). We shall look at the ethical implications of this in the next chapter; for now let us just focus on the element of self-affirmation.

We need to get a feeling for that shift in awareness that Nietzsche heralded. Under a fixed order, in which the value of everything is related to a given and accepted structure, we know our place, and hence we know what we should do. When that old order fades, however, we are at a loss to value ourselves or anything, unless we do so on the basis of our will. We do not say, to use Nietzsche's image, that the Superman *is* the meaning of the Earth, but that the Superman *shall be* the meaning of the Earth. *In other words, value is given by the will, not discovered out there in the world.*

If we try to give ourselves meaning and direction in terms of the ordinary things with which we are surrounded, we end up 'falling' into the world of the 'in-itself' (to use Sartre's term) or the 'being at hand' (in Heidegger). In other words, we start to see ourselves, not as beings whose key character is freedom and consciousness, but as things, trapped in their place by other things.

There is a wonderful moment in Camus' story 'The Adulterous Woman' when, going out into the night while staying in a desert town in North Africa, the wife of a tired and failing businessman looks up at the night sky. There – in an experience described in terms that resemble an orgasm – she finds herself totally at home beneath the stars in a vast and supremely beautiful universe. On returning to the hotel room and her sleeping husband, she lies down in the bed and weeps. There is a sense that her life has become so small, so confined to her very limited roles. Her adultery is not in a relationship with another man, it is in seeing herself as fully and authentically alive as a human being within a beautiful universe. The universe has brought her alive in a way her husband cannot.

All of that is a development of Nietzsche's saying 'yes' to life. And that has to be a 'yes' to a life that is finite – not one that somehow finds an external guarantee. For Nietzsche, the challenge of his 'eternal recurrence' is to say 'yes' to this life just as it is now, even if we knew that it would all be repeated over and over again for ever.

The essence of existential humanism, according to Sartre, is self-transcendence. In other words, at every moment, in every choice, a human being is able to become something more than what he or she was a moment before. We are constantly going beyond ourselves – a theme to which we shall return.

Masks and bad faith

The enemy of authentic living is, according to Sartre, *mauvaise foie* (bad faith). This can simply mean self-deception, or lying to oneself. But it is rather more than that, because to lie implies that one knows the truth; to lie to yourself is, therefore, an expression of a cynical, rather than a mistaken consciousness. But how is this expressed?

Here Sartre comes to our aid with another of his illuminating examples (in *Being and Nothingness*, p. 82). He observes a waiter in a café and sees that his actions are all a little too contrived, precise and rapid. He is actually a waiter in a café, but at the same time he is playing at being a waiter in a café. He is trying to follow a role, to act out his part perfectly, and therefore it all looks a bit strained. He is not being authentic, not being himself.

Similarly he argues that people expect a grocer, tailor or auctioneer to be nothing but that. They are expected simply to act out the role for us – we see them as 'things' in our world. Even more so the soldier, who is required to act the role without any thought of self, even to the point of putting his or her life at risk. Bad faith is accepting and pretending that one is nothing but that role, allowing oneself to be no more than a 'thing', part of the 'in-itself' world.

Of course, other people may need to see me in a role. I'm no use as a waiter unless I actually do my job. The situation becomes bad faith, and I slip into an inauthentic mode of being, when I myself accept myself as only acting within that role. In other words, it is the point at which I identify entirely with the social mask I wear.

Bad faith involved deliberately denying something we know to be true of ourselves; it is an attempt to escape from our own anxiety about the ambiguity of our lives. In other words, it is the point at which a person chooses to identify himself or herself entirely with his or her 'being-for-others'.

Notice what Sartre is doing here. He is using a practical example in order to make his point. You 'see' what the waiter is doing, and are therefore aware of the gap between the waiter and his reality. That is down to the method of phenomenology – exploring what is seen in our experience, rather than setting up a theoretical framework. Sartre has a wonderful way of using his literary talent to enable us to see what he sees and thereby understand what he means.

Similarly, in *Being and Time*, Heidegger sees the danger of doing as 'one' (*das Man*) does – in other words, following what is socially expected, rather than choosing for yourself how you will live – as an escape mechanism, avoiding the responsibility of choice. He also speaks of the 'fallenness', a state of being lost in the world of things and tasks and occupations, living exclusively by adopting the ready-made roles one is offered.

Of course, many will stay in this 'fallen' state rather than face the Angst of accepting freedom, responsibility and the challenge and uncertainty of an authentic life.

Key to escaping bad faith is the recognition that we are actually free. Only if we deny freedom do we slip back into a world of 'things' and bad faith, where everything we do appears to be the product of external causes and constraints.

The roles of women

One is not born a woman, but becomes one.

Simone de Beauvoir, *The Second Sex*

Simone de Beauvoir's *The Second Sex*, published in 1949, has been a hugely influential and very popular book, articulating the injustice of women's place in a world dominated by men and encouraging liberation and authenticity.

She explores the way women have been seen historically, and questions why they have accepted the role of being the 'second' sex, defined in terms of their relationship to men – as wife, mother, daughter, lover. There is a sense, seen perhaps in the assumptions of many characters in Jane Austen's novels, that a woman becomes somebody only when a man takes notice of her, and provides her with a role and a place in society. Long before de Beauvoir, Austen, George Eliot and others, were exposing this relative nature of women, and starting to affirm their heroines as women in their own right, independent of the social world created by men.

In *The Second Sex* she offers a *social* critique of the position in which women find themselves. They are prevented from adopting existentialist freedom because they are expected to conform to social views about what is expected of women. In other words, the temptation for an individual to live in bad faith, or to adopt a mask, is a *social phenomenon not simply an individual one*. Therefore, in order to effect change – even if that change happens one person at a time – there needs to be a change in the way that society as a whole views the place of women.

Gender is generated by the accepted conventions of society; it is part of the given in the world into which every female is 'thrown' at birth. And like all such conventions, it can be challenged and changed.

Key to her thinking is the central existential doctrine that existence precedes essence – in other words, a woman is what she makes of herself, she does not have some eternal, fixed essence to which she must conform. This is crucial, for if there is a distinctive feminine essence, women can be expected to adopt roles that reflect that essence. On the other hand, if existence comes first, then women are free to develop their own nature by the free choices that they make, unfettered by prior ideas of essence.

De Beauvoir's work highlights the balance between the individual and society and raises questions for existentialism: How do you change individuals without also changing the society within which they live? Are you personally responsible for living in bad faith, or wearing a mask, if that is the expectation of the society into which you are born?

If existentialism is about the courage to live an authentic life, shaking off traditional masks and affirming oneself in one's free choices, then it developed at exactly the right moment for women, and its impact on the social relations between the sexes has been deep-rooted and lasting.

Courage and reason

Heidegger, Sartre and de Beauvoir all see adopting an established role, or mask, as the easy way out. To be authentic, to be in the 'for-itself' mode, or to be a woman, requires courage and an attitude which accepts one's own situation and is willing to take responsibility for it.

Courage is often associated with facing the prospect of death. Heidegger makes the point that the inauthentic self (the *Man-selbst*) sees death as an event that will happen at some point in the future, but which does not trouble the present; in other words, it tries to avoid death as a possibility for my being here and now. One dies, but not yet. But from an existentialist perspective, death is the one certainty that is also indeterminate; we know *that* it will happen, but not *when*. Courage is facing that certainty and allowing it to give us a new perspective on our life, for it allows us to see ourselves as 'that is what I was'. To accept that (as we saw in terms of 'hell is other people') is never easy, for it is the only occasion when we are utterly exposed as we are, without the prospect of putting the record straight or claiming that we have a potential that is as yet undiscovered.

Courage is also required to step outside the comfort zone of reason. Authenticity requires that we deal with the immediate situation, not some absolute ideal. It is made more difficult because the world never fits in with our expectations, not what we think it should be. The problem is that we want to live reasonably in a world that is reasonable, but reality refuses to comply with our expectations. The existentialist rejects the rationalist presupposition, recognizing that we have to deal with the world just as it is, and take responsibility for the choices we make in it. We cannot excuse ourselves on the grounds that the world has not provided what we would have liked.

The absurd thing is that the world is not reasonable; indeed, we would have no reason to call the world absurd if we did not assume that a reasonable world would be at least possible. There is therefore a gap between the human longing to make sense of the world, and our experience of it.

The modern dilemma is that science shows us a world that is both reasonable (in the sense that it is predictable rather than capricious) and impersonal. That may be intellectually satisfying from the standpoint of an objective view of things – a study of the 'in-itself' – but it does not really help to address the existential questions, as the 'for-itself' courageously seeks to create meaning and value.

So courage is required to address a world that does not conform to one's reasonable expectations. There are some periods of history where courage, or the lack of it, is more clearly visible than others. Some (perhaps all) of the thinkers we have been examining battled with internal and personal dilemmas, but they also have in common the background of a world in a state of change or trauma.

Nietzsche's work probes the implications in changes of belief and attitude in nineteenth-century Europe. Heidegger's work has as its backdrop the trauma of the First World War, and the terrible state of the German economy in the 1920s. If he wanted to give individuals, the university and the German *Volk* a sense of courage and self respect, it was because he felt they were lacking, in a situation where it would be all too easy to be swamped by despair and nihilism.

Sartre studied Heidegger's *Being and Time*, and drafted his own *Being and Nothingness* while incarcerated in Stalag 12D prisoner-of-war camp, the quintessential setting for asking existential questions. A forged certificate, claiming disorientation due to partial blindness in his right eye, gained him his freedom to return to Paris where he wrote *Les Mouches* (*The Flies*), a pro-Resistance play, as well as finishing his *Being and Nothingness* and the first two volumes of his *Roads to Freedom* trilogy. This is no ivory tower philosophy, but one forged in a world under Nazi occupation, where courage was constantly in demand.

The existentialists were not provided with a comfortable, reasonable world.

6

freedom, choice and responsibility

In this chapter we shall be looking at what existential authenticity involves in terms of freedom, responsibility and ethics. I cannot choose the circumstances of my life, but I can choose how I will react to them. For Sartre, that gives me a measure of freedom and responsibility and establishes the personal challenge of existentialism.

Existential freedom is an experience – and a threatening one at that; it is quite separate from the question of whether, from an objective, scientific point of view, we are predictable. We cannot shelve our responsibility for what we do by blaming circumstances. We may not be able to achieve what we want, but we are always free to choose what we try to do.

So, for existentialists, morality is not a matter of accepting established traditions or being respectable, but of constructing the values by which they choose to live, but mindful that there is always going to be an 'ambiguity' in morality because of the freedom I experience and the circumstances within which I find myself.

What do you do when all the old certainties are removed, when the world presents itself as fragile, full of hazards, offering you an uncertain future or perhaps no future at all? What can you hold onto and commit to in a world where global financial crises may drain your savings or your future pension, where redundancy may threaten your lifestyle or take your home from you, when loved ones die, or friendships turn sour?

One option is to become a nihilist, to say that nothing has (or can have) value. Another is to take the less pessimistic but more challenging route of admitting that meaning and value are created rather than discovered, and to acknowledge that the choosing and committing is what gives life meaning. This was the option taken by Nietzsche and the majority of existentialist thinkers.

So the existentialist challenge was to reject external authority and all forms of social convention and to live purposefully in the light of your own values and self-understanding. That offers freedom, but also brings responsibility; taken seriously, it was never going to be an easy option.

Freedom: illusion or reality?

The problem of freedom is one that has long concerned philosophy. One may believe oneself to be free to choose, but from the standpoint of the external observer, that freedom is an illusion. The task of science is to find reasons for everything that happens. These may be physical, social or psychological. My therapist will assure me that my decision was quite predictable; an economist will see my decision to withdraw money from my bank as merely one example of an inevitable trend within the economy.

It is even theoretically possible that, at some point in the future, perhaps as a result of advances in neuroscience, we will be able to explain every choice in terms of antecedent neural activity. At that point, it might seem nonsense to speak of human freedom, or to ascribe praise or blame to any actions. But we do not need to wait for a perfect neuroscience to explain all aspects of human behaviour, we already relate criminality to social deprivation and violent behaviour to early upbringing. In court there are always mitigating circumstances. That might suggest that freedom is an illusion.

But all such views treat the self as an 'in-itself' (to use Sartre's term). In other words, they treat it as an object within the world of phenomena. But the freedom that is celebrated by existentialists is the freedom of the 'for-itself', the experience of freedom in choosing and acting to shape its own future. 'Man does not exist *first* in order to be free *subsequently*; there is no difference between the being of man and his being-free' (Sartre, *Being and Nothingness*, p. 49).

Kierkegaard described a kind of dizziness that came with the experience of free choice, a choice made in the context of (as the title of one of his books has it) 'Fear and Trembling'. Whatever philosophy and science may have to say about human freedom, it is certainly *experienced* as real, and that is what counts for existentialism.

But our relationship with freedom is ambivalent. Sartre saw man as 'a useless passion' because he was always wanting to be free, while at the same time wanting to find in himself some fixed essence and to identify himself with the objective 'in-itself' world.

For Sartre, we are 'condemned to be free'; it is not an option. We can only attempt to escape it by retreating back into the world of things (the 'in-itself'), denying the key feature of human consciousness.

In part IV of *Being and Nothingness,* Sartre gives useful summaries of his argument. He emphasizes that every act projects the self towards nothingness, towards what is not; in other words, the self sets itself goals, chooses what it wants to happen. Things may get in my way, but they cannot determine who I am or what I choose for myself. Freedom is not simply an *aspect* of being me, it is *what it means* to be me. I cannot be sometimes a slave and sometimes free – I am always free, whether I like to acknowledge it or not.

Now, one may well argue that I am not totally free; life does indeed provide me with limitations, I cannot do anything I want. Notice however that the freedom that Sartre insists on in *Being and Nothingness* is not the freedom to *achieve* what we want, but to *choose* what we want.

Responsibility

Responsibility is something you cannot escape. Kierkegaard made the important point that you have to take responsibility for making a choice, and that you are equally responsible if you refuse to make a choice, because you allow what happens to be determined by circumstances rather than by your act of will. Letting nature take its course is still a choice for which you are responsible.

According to Heidegger, it is always tempting to avoid responsibility by following 'das Man' (Man), in other words, by doing what is expected of you. But that is seen by existentialists as a cop out – we are free and responsible, and it is no good following orders or blaming circumstances.

This was expressed succinctly by Beckett in *Waiting for Godot*, where Vladimir says to Estragon: 'There's a man all over for you, blaming on his boots the faults of his feet.'

Therefore, whether we refer to it as adopting a mask, or living in bad faith, or inauthenticity, it amounts to the same thing – refusing to take personal responsibility and blaming our situation on the various 'boots' that we have, whether they be our background, economic circumstances, genetic predisposition, the limitations of the political situation, friends, family or whatever. They are all 'boots', whereas the existentialist will consider nothing but the responsibility of the feet within them.

If you think of yourself as nothing more than an object, science – in the form of psychology, sociology, economics or neuroscience – may offer you a perfect set of excuses for what you do. But for existentialists that would be to fall into 'bad faith'.

Perhaps the simplest way of looking at this is to say that existentialism challenges us to balance our dreams against our facts, neither using our circumstances as an excuse, nor detaching our dreams from reality.

At the end of his *The Phenomenology of Perception*, Merleau-Ponty highlights the existentialist claim that one must take responsibility by saying that it is: '... by plunging into the present and the world, by taking on deliberately what I am fortuitously, by willing what I will and doing what I do, that I can go further'.

And that encapsulates the essence of what the existential life is about; it is the position of affirmation from which I can move forward.

Constructing morality

In *Existentialism and Humanism*, Sartre sees moral choice as being like the construction of a work of art: it is the creative process of shaping our lives and thereby showing our values. You are free to choose what to do, and required to take responsibility for that choice. Morality, then, is something to be constructed.

But he also seems to come improbably near to promoting the ethics of Immanuel Kant, that great philosopher of the European Enlightenment and advocate of a supremely rational approach to life. Sartre argues that, in choosing for yourself you are in effect choosing for everyone else as well.

His argument here is very clear; it can be summed up in this way:
* If you act to create yourself, you also create an image of what you believe a man (or woman) should be;
* To make a choice is to affirm the value of what is chosen;
* We always choose what we see as better for us, and therefore, by implication, for everyone;
* As we choose, we shape an image that is valid for everyone;
* Hence our responsibility is great, because it concerns a choice for 'mankind as a whole'.

He concludes by claiming that: 'In fashioning myself I fashion man.' (*Existentialism and Humanism*, p. 33).

What cannot be in doubt, however, is that Sartre follows Nietzsche in his emphasis on the responsibility – in the absence of God – to choose values and live by them. The particular twist that Sartre gives to this process is that we act first and display our values through that action. We do not select who we want to be and then try to live up to it (that would lead to bad faith) but we shape ourselves, and thereby reveal our values: we are as we act. And that is what constitutes the seriousness of existentialist ethics; it is all down to us, there is no eternal set of values, no blueprint in the form of an ideal 'essence' of humankind to guide us.

Sartre himself was scathing of 'respectable' morality and values:

> **The bourgeois who call themselves 'respectable citizens' do not become respectable as the result of contemplating moral values. Rather from the moment of their arising in the world they are thrown into a pattern of behaviour the meaning of which is respectability. Thus respectability acquires a being; it is not put into question. Values are sown on my path as thousands of little real demands, like the signs which order us to keep off the grass.**

Being and Nothingness (p. 62)

To sink into respectability, to do what is expected, is to live in bad faith. To be authentic, to be a true existentialist, we should boldly forge our own values and lifestyle, constructing our own morality.

The problem with such existential morality is that, since there is no external value beyond what one creates through one's own commitments, the power of commitment becomes its own moral justification. (Nietzsche's advice was: 'Choose your own perspective, but live with the knowledge that such a perspective has no warrant but that of your will.') Yet, if that is so, how can we ever get a perspective from which to say what we all know, namely that people can sometimes be sincerely wrong and unwisely committed? How, if at all, can we get outside our own commitment and perspective? But that question takes us into the world of post-modernism...

One problem with existentialist ethics is that it appears to be centred on the individual, rather than on a concern for the welfare of all. Thus, for example, Iris Murdoch (in *The Sovereignty of Good*, p. 47) opposes existentialist ethics on the grounds that morality requires unselfishness, whereas she thinks that existentialism is always ego-bound. But key existentialist thinkers, including Sartre himself, themselves struggled with the social dimension. Thus, in *Existentialism and Humanism*, Sartre argues that one should strive not just for one's own freedom but for the freedom of all, and Jaspers feared that the value of philosophy would be lost if it remained hidden in the world of personal communication rather than engaging in the crucial issues of the day.

Nevertheless, there is a fundamental difference in approach between those (like Murdoch) who take a basically Platonic view of eternal values, and the values on which existential thought is based. Foundational values are not (for the existentialist) objectively given, they are created. We do not discover them, we create them. But in that case, what grounds do you have for prescribing such values to others, which is what moral claims appear to be doing?

If it is to escape accusations of being egocentric and self-indulgent, existentialism needs to link its view of authenticity to the general good of society. This is what Sartre attempted to do in his famous 1945 lecture, showing that existentialism stood within a genuinely humanist tradition.

The degree to which Sartre succeeded in that attempt to link his existentialism to traditional humanism is a matter of debate, not least because he himself was later to regret the position he took at that time. What we do know, however, is that existentialism insists that we are responsible for constructing and taking responsibility for our values and the commitments they reflect.

Far from being nihilist, existentialists take commitments seriously, selecting values and living by them. They refuse to conform to established norms simply because they do not want to become part of the impersonal world of the 'in-itself'.

The ethics of ambiguity

> *Ontology itself can not formulate ethical precepts. It is concerned solely with what is, and we can not possibly derive imperatives from ontology's indicatives.*

Sartre, *Being and Nothingness* (p. 645)

Clearly, there is always going to be a problem (referred to in philosophy as the 'naturalistic fallacy') of moving from 'is' to 'ought', but if existentialism describes what it is to be a human being, embedded in the world and yet always transcending it, that view of humankind is bound to have implications for how people understand themselves, and how they evaluate action. It was highlighted by the idea of authentic and inauthentic existence – so that, if existentialism cannot (and absolutely will not!) tell you what you ought to do, it will at least point out when you are being intellectually dishonest, or self-deceiving.

On the one hand existentialists see people as meaning-giving, free individuals who care nothing for what society expects or regards as the norm – a view that is reinforced by the popular image of the existentialist lifestyle. On the other, they want to affirm that people are subject to the look of others, that they live in society. This is the 'ambiguity' in existence to which both Merleau-Ponty and de Beauvoir refer.

In *The Ethics of Ambiguity* (1947) de Beauvoir presents an ethics that works within the general parameters of Sartrean existentialism, but it is given a more political and less individualist slant than in the work of Sartre himself.

We need to focus here on the nature of the ambiguity described by de Beauvoir. On the one hand, you have the human desire for freedom, for self-affirmation, for escaping social pressures to conform – all of those features that made existentialism so popular. On the other hand, every individual is located in a physical, social and political environment, with his or her life determined to a considerable extent by factors that are not within his or her control.

So any ethical argument must recognize this ambiguity, that one may be at one and the same time free, and yet constrained. To accept only the constraint is to kill off all freedom and live in bad faith; to accept only freedom is to be naïvely unrealistic and escapist.

It is also important to recognize that, for de Beauvoir, other people do not necessarily limit your own freedom but may actually be the means of making freedom possible. And freedom, of course, is not seen simply in terms of doing whatever you wish – that would be quite naïve – but in having a sense of a future in which one might freely choose between possibilities. And that may require a social movement rather than simply an individual vision.

Her view of ethics takes into account the social changes of the past; it is not simply an ethics of a moment of free existential decision. It also recognizes that one's own freedom may only be exercised in the context of the freedom of others – and indeed of a changed social situation in which, for example, an oppressed group can affirm themselves. And there will always be ways in which oppressors try to justify their oppression, perhaps in terms of the essence or natural qualities of the group whom they wish to keep in place. To liberate individuals in such a situation, it is necessary to change society.

7

the individual, art and society

The existentialists influenced (and were influenced by) trends in society and the arts. They celebrated authenticity in artistic expression wherever they found it.

From the anxiety which marks even Cezanne's solid-looking work to the anguished stick-like figures of Giacometti, the existentialists were able to point to the existential angst with which the artist struggled or that they sought to depict. Existentialists found in such art expressions of their view of the world.

This was also a time in which literary conventions and rules were being broken. From the free verse of T.S. Eliot's *The Waste Land* to the literary anarchy of James Joyce's *Ulysses*, or the breaking of chronological narrative in Marcel Proust's *In Search of Lost Time*, there was a sense that the writer should be free to express himself or herself.

This chapter offers a taster of the many literary and artistic parallels to existentialist philosophy.

Existentialists never had or wanted to have an ivory tower of any sort, academic or romantic. They were happy to live in the centre of modern cities, most notably in Paris, where they frequented street cafés abuzz with the latest ideas. Sartre called the magazine he founded in 1945 *Les Temps Modernes*. The title referred to Charlie Chaplin's satirical film *Modern Times* of 1936 that had attacked the modern industrial world. For Sartre it indicated on the contrary a determined acceptance of modernity. As philosophers go, existentialists were unusually aware of, and influenced by, the latest trends in society and the arts. The influence ran both ways. Existentialism affected the art of post-war Paris more than any other philosophical school has done. This was partly due to the exceptional atmosphere of Paris at the time.

When existentialism emerged in Paris in the 1940s, the city had been the centre of modern art for almost a century, home to successive radical movements: realism, Impressionism, Post-Impressionism, cubism, Fauvism and surrealism. It had become famed as the City of Light, attracting artists, writers and bohemians from across the world. (The term *bohemian* itself comes from *Scènes de la Vie de Bohème* of 1849 by Henri Murger, a writer who lived a true bohemian's life, dying in abject poverty. Puccini's famous opera *La Bohème* of 1896 was based on Murger's book.) Paris had also long been a beacon of political, social and intellectual freedom to people fleeing persecution of any sort. This reputation revived, albeit fragilely, after 1945. The 'School of Paris', the pre-war group of foreign artists that had included Chagall and Miró, was proudly re-established.

After 1945 New York steadily displaced Paris as the capital of the visual arts, but this was not at once apparent either in France or abroad. Foreign artists and writers – among them the Swiss-born sculptor and painter Alberto Giacometti (1901–66) and the Irish-born Samuel Beckett – still regarded Paris as their obvious home. It was still a city of unparalleled allure. The years after 1945 saw, besides the emergence of existentialism, the rebirth of French fashion (Dior's romantic New Look) and of French cinema (Jacques Tati's satirical films about modern society featuring

Monsieur Hulot). Both, if typically French in their charm, were traditional, even nostalgic in their outlook.

In the visual arts, however, a truly novel savagery and apparent ugliness emerged, *art brut* (literally: 'crude' or 'raw art'), involving materials like sand and great impasto daubs of paint. Jean Dubuffet, an artist and writer who had his first one-man exhibition in 1945, was the most articulate of its practitioners. 'The idea that there are beautiful objects and ugly objects, people blessed with beauty and others without it, surely rests only on convention – it's nonsense,' he wrote. 'I declare such conventions diseased... People notice that I aim to sweep away everything that we have been taught to think unquestioningly beautiful and graceful, but they overlook my efforts to substitute another, greater beauty, covering every being and object, including the most despised... I want people to look on my work as an attempt to rehabilitate scorned values... I am convinced that any table can for each of us be a landscape as inexhaustible as the whole Andes range.'

Only an art like Dubuffet's seemed to the existentialists to match the age that had begun in 1945, the age of Auschwitz and Hiroshima. But while unusually eloquent, Dubuffet was merely one among many French artist–propagandists.

Authentic experience: artists, writers and musicians

Most philosophers have tended to shy away from artists and writers. Whatever their own tastes in the creative arts, logical thinkers have often considered actual artists and poets unreliable bohemians. Not so the existentialists. The emaciated 'stick-like' figures of Alberto Giacometti quiver with a tension and anguish which was quickly recognized as typically existentialist. Sartre first met Giacometti in 1939 just as the artist was beginning to evolve his utterly original style after going through a surrealist phase.

For existentialism, a philosophy that called on human beings to define themselves through their actions, artistic creativity was always supremely important. Sartre saw in the artist who produces original work from nothing a paradigm of authentic human existence. 'In life a man commits himself, draws his own portrait and there is nothing but that portrait', he wrote. 'As everyone knows, there are no aesthetic values *a priori*... no one can tell what a painting tomorrow will be like.' This emphasis on the new-created – of which there can be no prior (*a priori*) knowledge, and so no aesthetic rules – underlay much of existentialism's appeal to avant-garde artists.

Clearly, existence precedes essence applies to art as much as to human reality; in art, as in life, we are challenged to create our own aesthetic values.

Well before Sartre began extolling his contemporaries in the 1940s, he had been interested in modernism. He saw its struggles as complementing his own literary and philosophical efforts, aptly for a thinker who spent most of his life in Paris. At the beginning of the twentieth century the cubists' radical fracturing of form had led to the destruction of single-viewpoint linear 'mathematical' perspective. Linear perspective had underpinned all Western art since the fifteenth-century Renaissance, giving it the seemingly objective assurance that helped make Western art unmistakeably 'Western'. But from now on it was possible, even required, for artists to depict objects from multiple viewpoints, as if seen simultaneously from several angles, as if there were no 'correct' way of looking at anything. Each artist could – must – create the visual world afresh.

This revolution, initiated by Picasso and Braque following in Cézanne's footsteps, was a response to perceived artistic, not intellectual, problems and long predated existentialism. *Les Demoiselles d'Avignon* (or *The Brothel*, as Picasso candidly first called it) the prototypical cubist work, was painted in 1907, although Picasso did not exhibit it in public until 1916, aware of its explosive potential. It is still startling today, as much for its savage energy and novel ugliness inspired by non-European art as for its disregard of linear perspective. More than any other work, it signalled the advent of a new aesthetics.

The new aesthetics was evident in the other arts. T.S. Eliot, who lived for a time in Paris, pioneered 'free verse', most famously in *The Waste Land* (1922), often considered the twentieth-century's archetypal poem. 'Free prose' was probably pioneered by Gertrude Stein, another American resident in Paris who wrote maddeningly repetitive prose, but its time genius was James Joyce, an Irish writer, also living in Paris after 1918. Joyce's bewildering, exhilarating polyphonic novel *Ulysses* of 1922 broke all rules, including those on obscenity. (For these reasons the novel could not be published in the Irish Republic for more than 40 years.)

From now on chronological narrative, the backbone of the nineteenth-century novel, seemed incidental, almost redundant. In Marcel Proust's immense novel *In Search of Lost Time* (*A la Recherche du Temps Perdu*, 1909–22), time itself dissolves to become a mirror-like maze through which the narrator wanders, half in entranced reverie, half in caustic observation.

A similar revolution shattered the world of classical music. The primitive pulsations of Stravinsky's ballet *The Rite of Spring* (*Le Sacré du Printemps*), premiered in Paris in 1913, marked a crucial change in Western music, from all-resolving final harmony to spiky, savagely driving rhythm. Traditional musical form could never be the same again. If a lot of classical music did not continue far in this direction, jazz, which arrived in Paris from the USA in the 1920s, certainly did. Modernism, while elitist in its disdain for public opinion, was relentless in its attack on old hierarchies.

This artistic 'revaluation of all values' (Nietzsche's words) presaged the total psychological and social uprooting that the two world wars confirmed in politics. By 1945 a process that had started gently with the Impressionists – who chose to paint scenes of everyday life, such as streets, river banks and domestic interiors, rather than officially favoured grand historical or religious subjects – was producing an art of strident *angoisse* (anguish) well suited to existentialism. If the novels by Sartre, Camus and de Beauvoir proved conventional enough in narrative form, their contents were truly radical, exciting readers around the world.

As de Beauvoir wrote, 'France, having become a second class power, defended itself by glorifying its exports, Fashion and Literature.'

Cézanne, master of anxiety

The years immediately after 1945 saw renewed admiration for Paul Cézanne among the avant-garde in Paris. This might seem a little odd for a painter who had by then been dead for nearly 40 years. Cézanne had died in 1906 aged 68 and his posthumous fame had steadily grown until he was widely regarded as the greatest artist of his age. In Cézanne's wonderful landscapes of Mont Ste-Victoire or his still lifes of apples and bottles, he seemed to have grasped the very essence of objects, be they mountains or fruits, painting form with a passionate lucidity.

Yet Cézanne's time-defying, quasi-geometrical art – seeing in nature 'the cylinder, the sphere, the cone' as he put it – was achieved only at huge personal cost and repeated professional disappointments. Looked at again, his apples, tables and bottles almost burst from their canvases with tension and stress; the sharp rocks of his Provençal mountains jut out restlessly as if into a fourth dimension. Acute personal nervousness underlies all his monumental paintings, not just his 'morbid' early works. It was this *angoisse* which appealed to the existentialists, who acclaimed the painter as a suffering hero of the easel precisely because of his neuroses.

In 'Cézanne's Doubt' (La doute de Cézanne), an article of December 1945, Merleau-Ponty hailed Cézanne as a proto-existentialist. 'If painting was his world and his existence, anxiety was the basis of his character', wrote Merleau-Ponty, detecting in Cézanne's art 'a morbidity... schizophrenia... a flight from the world of humanity'. To Merleau-Ponty, at least at this stage in his thinking, as well as to other existentialists, such morbidity was potentially fruitful, for 'there is a connection between the schizoid constitution and Cézanne's work because his work reveals a metaphysical sense of his illness. If we regard schizophrenia as a state of mind in which the world is reduced to the sum of all its physical experiences but as if frozen, as a suspension of expressive values, then [mental] illness, in Cézanne's case, is no longer just absurd and ill-fated but opens up valid possibilities for all human existence.'

Merleau-Ponty's analysis – whether or not accurate about Cézanne, who if morbidly shy was never considered mentally ill – echoed Freud's famous psychoanalysis of Leonardo da Vinci. (This itself is now known to be flawed owing to a then common fallacy about Leonardo's infancy, but it was admired at the time.) The immediate heirs of Cézanne were the cubists, who carried his geometrical revolution to its conclusion.

Existentialist artists

From cubism a convoluted line runs – with a detour via Dadaism, that most nihilist of movements, and surrealism, the most flamboyant – to *art brut*. This school of art emerged at the same time, and as a response to the same circumstances, as existentialism. 'Raw art' was supposedly best made by psychotics – prisoners and others on society's extreme fringes – but in reality its practitioners soon became part of the art world. The actual term was coined by Dubuffet, who claimed that such art 'sprang from pure invention and was in no way based, as cultural art constantly is, on chameleon or parrot-like processes'. Instead it reveals an aggressive originality that everyone possesses but which is too often stifled by education and social constraints.

Bram van Velde (1895–1981), a Dutch-born artist who arrived in Paris in 1936 to fall deeply under Picasso's influence, wrote in 1948: 'Only those who are sick can be artists. It is their suffering which drives them to do the things that restore meaning to the world. The sensitive man or artist can only be sick in our civilized life filled with lies... Painting is man confronting catastrophe... I paint my misery.' Van Velde had no commercial success despite praise from Samuel Beckett, which may in part explain his misery.

Misérabiliste was the name of the style associated with Dubuffet and especially with Francis Gruber (1912–48), a French artist who died of TB. Gruber's mature style exudes a wintry melancholy, whether his subject is a nude, still life or landscape. Typical is *Job*, painted in 1944 and exhibited at the Salon d'Automne (the key annual exhibition) that year. Depicting the Old Testament character sorely tested by God, Gruber's Job, seated gaunt and nude on a stool in silent contemplation, symbolized the existentialist despair of the oppressed people of Paris, who yet retained their ultimate faith in their liberation. Gruber was from the start a politically committed painter, a Communist at a time when most existentialists were not.

Sartre championed Wols as the purest example of an existentialist artist, however. Wols was the pseudonym of the German-born Alfred Schulze (1913–51), who had studied at the Bauhaus, the modernist seminary in Weimar Germany, before moving to France in 1932 to escape the Nazis. After working initially as a photographer, he had his first solo show as a painter in December 1945. Soon he was producing highly original abstract works that rivalled, albeit on a smaller scale, those of contemporary American abstract expressionists. Despite Sartre's support, Wols lived in abject poverty, a situation he seemed almost to relish.

Sartre, who had first met Wols in 1945, recalled that he was 'bald with a bottle and a beggar's slouch…at 33 one would have thought him 50, had it not been for the youthful sadness in his eyes. Everyone thought that he would not make old bones. In the end his friends had to carry him in the evening to the Rhumerie Martinique [a bar] and bring him back in the middle of the night, a little more dead each day, a little more visionary.' Wols illustrated several of Sartre's books – usually in drypoint (black and white engraving on copper) – with designs of a savagery that thrilled the philosopher.

The artist most intimately connected with the existentialists themselves was the sculptor Alberto Giacometti, who made numerous portraits of de Beauvoir. Sartre in *The Search for the Absolute*, his introduction to the New York exhibition of 1948 that finally established Giacometti's reputation, hailed him as the age's greatest artist. He declared that Giacometti's only true rivals were the Palaeolithic artists of Altamira, not any twentieth-century contemporaries. (On visiting these famous cave paintings in northern Spain earlier, Picasso had said: 'After Altamira, all is decadence'.) Sartre himself wrote: 'After 3,000 [sic] years, the task of Giacometti and of contemporary sculptors is not to enrich the galleries with new works, but to prove that sculpture itself is still possible... there is a definite goal to be attained, a single problem to be solved: how to mould a man in stone without petrifying him.'

Merleau-Ponty in his 1961 essay *Eye and Mind* asserted that Giacometti's understanding of 'resemblance' was close to his own phenomenological approach. 'Resemblance is the result of perception, not its origin,' he wrote. Merleau-Ponty differentiated between *habitual* perception, based on knowledge accumulated over time, and *authentic* perception which, like the vision of a newborn child, precedes knowledge. Giacometti frequently used the same models – often members of his family – for his emaciated figures, but he claimed to look at them afresh each time. He said of his brother Diego Giacometti: 'He has posed ten thousand times for me, but the next time he poses I won't recognize him.'

Despite ever-growing success – in 1962 he won the grand prize for sculpture at the Venice Biennale – Giacometti led a frugal, even ascetic existence, reputedly living off black coffee and hard-boiled eggs. As de Beauvoir later said of him: 'Success, fame, money – Giacometti was indifferent to them all.'

A similar, genuinely bohemian indifference was exhibited by jazz musicians such as Boris Vian, who was also a poet, satirist and actor. In the late 1940s Vian, along with singers like Juliette Gréco (born 1927), used to perform in the small cellar night-clubs of Saint-Germain-des-Prés on the Left Bank, often underneath the very cafés where Sartre and company were debating. Jazz, after being banned under the German occupation, still seemed alluringly new. This milieu attracted among others the American writer James Baldwin, who found in it an escape from the racism and homophobia then prevalent in the USA. (A different, jaundiced view of French intellectual life came from the waspish American playwright Truman Capote. He described Sartre as 'wall-eyed, pipe-sucking, pasty-faced' and de Beauvoir as a 'spinsterish moll', the two 'propped up in a corner like an abandoned pair of ventriloquist's dolls'.)

existentialism
and religion

In this chapter we shall explore the idea that religion is concerned with fundamentally existentialist questions concerning the value and meaning life. Existentialist thinkers were divided between those, like Sartre, who were atheist, and others who were religious, even if unconventionally so.

Among theologians influenced by existential ideas, Bultmann showed that the scriptures should be interpreted in terms of their emotional and personal impact, rather than their factual content, and Tillich argued that God was not a being among others in the world, but was 'Being-itself' and our 'ultimate concern' – terms that had been used by Heidegger.

Whereas on the old, dualist way of thinking, God could be thought of as somehow external to us – a being who might or might not exist – the implication of existentialist interpretations of religion is to see 'God' as a way of describing the ultimate point of reference in our quest to find value and meaning in human life, in the face of our own transience and fragility.

Religion has always been existentialist. That may seem a curious statement to those who see existentialism as attempting to overthrow all traditional philosophy, and with it the metaphysics upon which religious beliefs have generally been based. But religion is not simply a matter of accepting certain beliefs. Religion is first and foremost a way of life, a commitment, a way of seeing and valuing. That way of life is expressed through beliefs, but it is generally true to say that for a religious person, those beliefs are not accepted in a detached or impersonal way, but are the basis of a personal engagement.

So religion focuses exactly on those things with which existentialism is concerned – commitment, choice and making sense of a life that is finite and ambiguous.

We find the origin of existential issues being discussed in the earliest religious traditions. Karl Jaspers describes as the 'axial age' a period from about 550 BCE when humankind started to move away from a mythological form of thinking to ask existential questions about the meaning and fragility of human life. From that age we have the Hebrew prophets, the earliest Greek thinkers, Confucius, Lao Tzu and the Buddha.

It is also widely recognized that, within the Christian tradition, Saint Augustine (354–430) explored the significance of Christianity in existential terms. He spoke of the depth of the self and its restless longings, of experiencing the self in terms of past, present and future, and exploring the place of religion in giving what one might now refer to as authenticity. The same could be said of many other religious figures. Luther, Kierkegaard and nineteenth-century revivalism all exemplified the religious demand for existential commitment.

So it is hardly surprising that, when it comes to twentieth-century existentialism, we find a range of attitudes towards religion.

The religious divide

Since Sartre, the key figure in twentieth-century existentialism, was an atheist, there is a tendency to assume that atheism is the existentialist norm. But this is neither logical nor true to the historical record. Many existentialist thinkers were religious, even if unconventionally so.

This is illustrated by those two great precursors of the existentialist movement, Kierkegaard and Nietzsche: the one profoundly religious, the other defiantly atheist. But that division continued within what we would think of as the mainstream of existentialist thinkers. Merleau-Ponty and Marcel were Catholic, Buber was Jewish, whereas Sartre, de Beauvoir and Camus were atheist.

But this simple division is not very helpful. Kierkegaard, seen as representing the religious tradition, fought against the conventional religious attitudes of his day, while Nietzsche, in his atheism, had an intensity and a commitment to human transcendence which has religious characteristics. Karl Jaspers was hardly a conventional religious believer, describing his position as one of having 'philosophical faith', and yet his views are profoundly religious, and he saw the striving of the secular philosopher as parallel to that of the believer.

Let us just say that existential questions are bound up with the same quest for self-understanding that lies behind religion – not the religion of beliefs and dogmas (a religion that has degenerated from a 'for-itself' to an 'in-itself', to use Sartre's terminology), but that which explores personal meaning and direction at a level that transcends the mundane.

In addition, there were a number of theologians who developed clearly existentialist ways of interpreting religious ideas. Bultmann, Tillich and Barth, major figures in twentieth-century theology, all used existential themes and language.

Probably the best way to understand how existentialism can come in both theistic and atheistic forms is to go back to the experience of radical contingency – the awareness that neither we nor anything else needs to exist; we are not our own explanation; we do not generate our own life; we might just as easily not exist at all.

From an atheist point of view, this fact of contingency is just a given feature of life. Because there is no external guarantor of meaning, we are challenged to give our own lives meaning by our choices and by affirming ourselves and striving for authenticity. But focus for a moment on that experience of contingency. I need not exist, but I *do exist*. My life does not provide its own explanation – it is just given to me, I have been 'thrown' (to use Heidegger's term) into this world. That can lead to a sense that the world is meaningless and absurd. But it can equally lead to the sense that the world is freely 'given', with a natural response in terms of gratitude, that, in spite of all the odds, I do actually exist. I have not created myself, but nevertheless I am here.

There is a tension, going back to the writings of Kierkegaard, between the limitations of each human being, and the impulse to somehow go beyond, to transcend. It sets the agenda for existentialist ethics, and also for a religious interpretation of existential themes. The religious existentialist focuses on this transcendence as a religious impulse.

Bultmann and Tillich

Heidegger moved to the University of Marburg in 1923, where he started writing *Being and Time*, finishing and publishing it in 1927. At Marburg he worked briefly alongside two theologians who were to display profoundly existential themes in their work: Rudolph Bultmann and Paul Tillich. The three were never close colleagues, and the only contact between Heidegger and Tillich was said to be through students who moved between their lectures, but Heidegger's work was still influential.

Bultmann, in his work on the New Testament, pointed out that the biblical narratives should not be taken in a literal sense, but as stories that were concerned to produce a response in their hearers (or later, their readers). Texts were written for a purpose and should be seen in the context in which they were originally used – they should not be mistaken for simple, factual accounts.

There is a huge and important issue at stake here, one that has profound implications for the nature of religion. If religious language is taken literally, a person stands in the wrong relationship to it.

The world, and individual events within it, can be examined scientifically. We may analyse events to see how they are caused and so on. Some events may be inexplicable, for some we may have insufficient evidence to know whether the accounts we have of them are correct or not. But the issue of the truth or otherwise of any statements at that factual level is of intellectual interest only.

Factual statements and proofs do not challenge us at a personal level. For that to happen, you need to get behind the factual to engage with stories that speak of the meaning and purpose of life.

So how does this relate to the New Testament, or indeed to belief in God? At one level, it is possible simply to examine textual evidence for how the scriptures came to be written, or to examine and weigh up rational arguments for or against belief in God. But these things do not in themselves engage us as human beings. I may study and know every word in the New Testament without thereby becoming religious.

So Bultmann and others took the step that had already been explored in the nineteenth century by Kierkegaard. They pointed out that what mattered was the existential interpretation of narratives, not their factual content.

The younger man, Paul Tillich — who was to produce his *Systematic Theology* in New York while Sartre was promoting existentialism in Paris — argued that God is characterized by two things:

* God is 'Being-itself', not a particular being
* God is 'ultimate concern'

Both concepts relate to the work of Heidegger, and both are key to an existentialist approach to religion. Tillich emphasized that the idea of God is related to the whole nature of our experience of Being — he cannot be simply one among other things that we encounter in the world. And just as Heidegger saw our involvement in the world as a matter of our 'concern', Tillich saw the word 'God' as indicating our ultimate concern, the commitment and challenge to deal with life as a whole.

The crucial thing to recognize with Tillich's thought is that what most people think of as 'God' – namely a being who might or might not exist 'out there' somewhere – is a modern form of idolatry. It is not just that such a God does not exist, which is the rather unnecessary argument put out by many atheists, but that the very idea of such a God deflects attention from the real object of religion, namely 'Being itself'.

Being itself is beyond existence and non-existence. So, in *Systematic Theology*, Tillich is able to say that 'God does not exist', because to say that he exists is to make him an object among objects, and that is idolatry. His own way of describing God is as 'the ground of our being', an idea taken up by John Robinson in *Honest to God*, the book that challenged conventional religious ideas in the 1960s.

It is difficult to overstate the significance of this shift within religious thought. Too often neglected since the days of radical theology in the 1960s and 70s, it provided an intellectual framework for ideas that may be traced back to Augustine, Luther, Kierkegaard and many other religious thinkers. Its neglect leads to the often sad confrontation between fundamentalist believers and equally fundamentalist atheists – twin forms of modern idolatry.

Shifting the idea of 'God'

Remember the basic structures by which Heidegger analysed Dasein – that we exist as a self-in-the-world, and that the world, for us, is a framework of meaning and significance. We engage with it all the time, our experience coloured by our mood.

Now think back to the very opposite of all this – to Descartes or the empiricists. They held that there was a fundamental division between mind and matter. Mind was 'in here' doing the thinking, while the world was 'out there' to be examined by science. All that we could know of the world was transmitted to us via our senses, and we had to judge the extent to which we could be certain about the information they gave.

So when we make the shift to Heidegger's ontology and its existentialist implications, we find that it sets a whole new agenda in terms of religious belief. On the old, dualist way of thinking, there could be a debate about whether or not God existed – in other words, whether there was something external to ourselves that corresponded to the word 'God'. And the philosophy of religion has a long history of examining arguments about that.

But look what happens once you adopt the existentialist perspective. God is no longer thought of as 'a being' alongside others, but 'being itself'. God becomes the ultimate point of reference in that web, or network of meaning that I call 'world' and within which I am embedded.

Even though, as we have seen, many existentialists were confirmed atheists, religion, in the broad sense of that word, can make sense from an existential perspective since it offers values and commitments which may help people to 'transcend' their narrow self-interest. 'God', in such an existential approach to religion, becomes a term for the ultimate framework of meaning and value within which we find ourselves.

The division within existentialism between the religious and the atheists is really quite fundamental. Consider this:

If you believe that meaning and value are not to be found within the world that you experience and within which you are embedded, you may see it as your responsibility to construct your own values, to live forwards towards the future that you choose for yourself and your world. That is a basically atheist position, and it reflects the central appeal of the work of Sartre.

On the other hand, if you believe that life offers us opportunities to *discover* meaning and value in the world, rather than simply *impose* them on it, you may (or you may not) want to express that sense of 'Being Itself' in terms of 'God'. Like the atheist, you may take your commitments seriously, you may recognize your responsibility to shape the future, but it is all done in the context of a relationship with the sense you have of a source of meaning outside yourself.

authenticity and the absurd: the fiction of Sartre and Camus

In this final chapter we turn to a feature of existentialism that gives it a very special place within the history of ideas: the way in which it found expression in fiction and drama.

Both Sartre and Camus explored the absurd and authenticity in their writings, drawing into their narratives all the key existentialist themes: that we are thrown into our particular situation in life; that we face death; that we affirm ourselves in the decisions we make; that we become who we are through our actions.

Existentialist themes are found most obviously in the literary works of Sartre, de Beauvoir and Camus, but are also explored by others, including Samuel Beckett, whose play *Waiting for Godot* raises profound existential questions, and the plays of Harold Pinter and Tom Stoppard.

From among the many works that illustrate and embody existential themes, we shall look at three by Sartre – a short story (*The Wall*) a novel (*Nausea*) and a play (*No Exit*) – and Camus' novels *The Outsider* and *The Plague*.

At any street corner the feeling of absurdity can strike a
person in the face.

Camus, *The Myth of Sisyphus*

Several existentialists were novelists and playwrights as
well as philosophers and two were outstanding. Both are still
read around the world and both were offered the Nobel Prize for
Literature (there is no prize for philosophy): Albert Camus, who
humbly accepted the prize in 1957, and Jean-Paul Sartre, who
proudly refused it in 1964 lest it jeopardize his independence.
For the general reader, the fiction of both is often the most
illuminating way to approach their philosophy. There is of course
one notable difference between Sartre and Camus: the former was
a great systematic philosopher who wrote major books of pure
philosophy, most notably *Being and Nothingness* (1943); the latter
only produced two short philosophical works, *The Myth of Sisyphus*
(1942) and *The Rebel* (1951). However, both were superb novelists,
exploring in fiction crucial themes of authenticity, freedom,
responsibility, bad faith and the Absurd.

There are occasions when only literature can fully convey
the subtle intricacies and dilemmas of the human condition.
For Sartre and Camus, fiction at times clearly offered the best way
to deal with the realities of the human condition *intellectually*.
Sartre's first great novel *Nausea* (*La Nausée*, published 1938)
gives a terrifying if marvellous sense of the contingency and
absurdity of human life. There is no need for any technical
philosophical language to appreciate the poetic heights – or tragic
depths – of it or his other novels, *The Roads to Freedom* trilogy,
or of Camus' *The Outsider* (*L'Étranger*) and *The Plague* (*La Peste*).
Sartre's plays such as *No Exit* (*Huis Clos*) have also entered the
repertory. This chapter investigates existentialism as it is
expounded through the fiction of Sartre and Camus.

The Wall

Sartre wrote many short stories from an early age. One was
recognized as a masterpiece from the moment of its publication
in *La Nouvelle Revue Française* in 1937, *The Wall* ('*Le Mur*'). It was

hailed by the critic Gaëtan Picon as 'pure, naked and full'. Set during the Spanish Civil War (1936–9), *The Wall* focuses on the psychology of three prisoners condemned to death without trial and awaiting execution at dawn. Through them, Sartre explores differing reactions to the knowledge of imminent death. (We all know that we will die, of course, but dismiss it as an unthinkably distant event.) The wall of the title is the wall against which the three men will be lined up and shot, into which the bullets will lodge after smashing through their bodies, the wall which they wish they could 'get inside' to escape the volleys. It also symbolizes the fixed limit set to every life.

Pablo Ibbieta is the narrator, an unheroic one despite his determination to 'die cleanly'. He looks without sympathy at Juan, the youngest of the prisoners sobbing pathetically. When Juan asks the doctor watching them, 'Does it [being shot] hurt much?' he gets an evasive reply. Ibbieta himself is sweating with a fear he does not like to acknowledge, while Tom the third prisoner wets his pants in terror. Ibbieta's mood in the cell is deeply nihilistic as he looks back on a life which 'was worth nothing because it was finished. I wondered how I had been able to walk, to laugh with girls; I wouldn't have moved as much as my little finger if I had ever imagined I would die like this.'

Ibbieta finds the Fascist officers interrogating him absurd, not intimidating. 'These men all dolled up with their riding crops and boots were still going to die. A little later than me, but not much... Their petty activities seemed shocking and burlesque to me... I couldn't put myself in their place.' Here Sartre stresses the existential truth that, seen in the light of eternity (*sub specie aeternatis*, as Spinoza put it), all our actions are essentially futile. Exactly when people are busying themselves with causes they think important enough to justify killing others, they are at their most absurd.

Offered his life by the Fascists in exchange for information about Gris, another wanted Republican, Ibbieta at first refuses. Then, to annoy his captors and buy time, he gives what he thinks is false information: Gris is hiding in the cemetery. Finding himself to his amazement reprieved, he hears from a man newly arrested that Gris has been found and shot. Gris had moved from his original hiding place – to the cemetery. 'I laughed so much I cried', Ibbieta says, and the story ends abruptly, discordantly.

Nausea

Sartre wrote *Nausea* (published in 1938) over six years, mostly while working as a philosophy teacher in Le Havre, a job he disliked but to which he returned after studying in Germany. The port is the model for Bouville, the novel's dismal setting. *Nausea* had great immediate success, enabling its author to move permanently back to Paris. It can be read at two levels: as an expression in fictional form of Sartre's metaphysical thought, anticipating theories developed in *Being and Nothingness*; or, in a literary sense, as an exploration of the problems of writing about a character writing a journal about doing nothing.

The novel is written as the journal of Antoine Roquentin, a gloomily introspective 30-year-old recluse who could be Sartre's alter ego. Returning to Bouville after years away, Roquentin is supposedly doing research for his biography of the Marquis de Robellon, an obscure eighteenth-century figure whose papers are in the local museum. In practice he simply wanders around the town thinking about the lack of meaning or purpose in his life.

Living almost completely alone, he experiences time as an endless caravan of dreary days passing. 'Nothing happens while you live. The scenery changes, people come in and go out, that's all... Days are tacked onto days without rhyme or reason, an interminable, monotonous addition.' Roquentin lives in a cheap hotel room, has almost no possessions and attempts only the most desultory writing. Even his memories of the past are jejune. 'However much I trawl through the past, I can only recover scraps of images and I don't know what they represent, nor if they are remembered or invented.'

Knowing that the future does not really exist – a knowledge most of us deny under the delusion that the future will somehow make us 'complete' – fills Roquentin with nausea. Nausea is the horrifying sense of the total contingency and absurdity of our existence. It attacks him like a vicious migraine and pervades everything. 'Nausea is not inside me: I feel it out there in the wall ... everywhere around me. It makes itself one with the café, I am the one who is *within it*.'

One of his nausea attacks is triggered by seeing in Bouville Museum portraits of dead burghers that depict them as taller and nobler – less contingent – than the Victorian haut bourgeois ever actually were. Typical of the type Roquentin hates is the 'handsome, impeccable' Jean Pacôme, whose 'magnificent grey eyes had never been clouded by the smallest doubt. Nor had Pacôme ever made a mistake.' Another bout of nausea is caused by an inoffensive old chestnut tree in a park. Its softness, stickiness and corpulence strike Roquentin as disgustingly, excessively *en soi* (in-itself, like all objects) and flabbily feminine in its 'soft, monstrous masses in disorder – naked, with a frightening, obscene nakedness'. (There is a misogynistic streak in Roquentin stemming perhaps from his author.)

Ultimately his nausea stems from grasping the mysteriously *contingent* existence of the universe as a whole, a realization that most human activities are implicitly designed to avoid. Roquentin in fact has had a quasi-mystical vision, albeit one of despair.

There is one other significant character in Bouville, Ogier P, whom Roquentin calls the Autodidact. A passionate socialist and humanist, he is trying to acquire all human knowledge available in the local library, learning facts by heart in alphabetical order. Devoid of personal charm and friends, he tries to befriend Roquentin but only provokes a new attack of nausea in him. Towards the novel's end, the Autodidact is caught stroking a schoolboy's hand in the library. Punched in the face, he is thrown out by the attendant and barred from the library, so ruining his life. Roquentin feels a sudden flash of pity for the Autodidact but his belated offer of help is refused.

Although a recluse, Roquentin has, or had, a girlfriend, Anny. She lives in Paris and dreams of their having 'perfect moments' together that they somehow never achieve. The thought of seeing her again after long separation fills him with unusual excitement and their reunion is described with touching honesty, free of sentimentality. Although Anny is now older and fatter, he finds himself falling in love again, but she declares that she has 'outlived herself' and developed an attitude to life that mirrors his. Unable to offer her any hope or reason for living, they part for good although still half in love. Back in Bouville, Roquentin realizes he is now utterly alone. Refusing to yield to what would be (for him) the luxury of total despair, Roquentin decides to leave Bouvillle and write a novel. Doing so will both justify his existence and distract him from it.

Nausea remains an astonishing novel. Though rooted in the French realist tradition, it bears comparison with Dostoyevsky's almost pathologically intense works such as *Notes from Underground* and *Crime and Punishment*. William Barrett wrote in *Irrational Man: A Study in Existential Philosophy* that *Nausea* 'may well be Sartre's best book for the very reason that in it the intellectual and the creative artist come closest to being conjoined'. If Sartre had written nothing else, he would still be remembered as a great author.

No Exit

Sartre's play *No Exit* (*Huis Clos*, also called *In Camera* or *Behind Closed Doors*) opened in May 1944 at the Théâtre du Vieux-Colombier in Paris. It was a great success, its message resonating in a city still under German occupation. It contains Sartre's most famous line, 'Hell is other people' (*L'enfer c'est les autres*). This is not as misanthropic as it sounds when seen in context, for the context is hell.

The play opens with a servant ushering Joseph Garcin into a claustrophobic over-furnished room without windows or mirrors. It becomes clear that Garcin is dead and in hell. Surprised to see no instruments of torture, he is informed by the servant that sleep – even closing one's eyes – is impossible and there is no way out, no relief or distraction from the relentless pressure of eternal reality. A hellish prospect, but reality involves other people and into the room are ushered in sequence two women: Inès Serrano, a lesbian postal clerk and Estelle Rigault, a vacuous society blonde. After their entry, the door is closed and locked. None has had any earlier connection with the others but all are now condemned to their mutual company for eternity. They are also doomed to torture each other mentally. (Each represents a significantly different stratum of the bourgeoisie: Garcin is a bourgeois intellectual, Inès a petty bourgeois clerk, Estelle a rich bourgeois.)

All, as they question one other, finally reveal why they are there: Garcin is a coward, an army deserter, cruelly unfaithful to his wife; Inès has driven another woman to suicide by manipulating and taunting her; Estelle has drowned a baby she had by her lower-class lover. Each is desperate to win over one of the others: Garcin wants the good opinion of Inès, who is trying to seduce Estelle, who is trying to seduce Garcin... Their bickerings intensify until Garcin suddenly demands an exit. 'Open the door! Open, damn you! I'll suffer anything, red-hot tongs, molten lead... anything is better than this mental agony.' But when the door suddenly flies open, he refuses to move. So does Inès. She too is a coward, he discovers.

The point of this blackest of comedies is not to depict an afterlife that makes oblivion seem enticing but to examine a key aspect of our life on earth: the existence of other people and the crippling effect this can have on us when we are 'being-for-others'. Subject to the judgement and freedom of the Other, we are at their mercy, 'enslaved' in Sartre's words. In short, hell is indeed other people – at least in such an infernal room without windows, books, sleep, darkness, work, tears, nature or any other escape.

Camus' novels

Camus' fiction rivals Sartre's in its intellectual power and, for many readers, surpasses it in literary appeal. In a way his work stands at an opposite pole to Sartre's. Its final note is not one of Sartrean disgust and nausea at existence but of rejoicing in physical reality despite everything. Camus' novels, like his plays and essays, wrestle with a central dilemma: Is life worth living in a universe that strips us of all significance, or is suicide the honest solution? He reached a positive but tough-minded conclusion: Yes, life is worth the struggle but only if we are prepared to face both its absurdity and our own consequent futility. Conor Cruise O'Brien, an often unsympathetic critic, conceded that 'to a generation which saw no reason for hope, it [Camus' work] offered hope without reason... it allowed the joy of being alive in the presence of death to emerge'.

Camus could view life on the shores of his native Mediterranean ecstatically and was wonderful at evoking the physical joys of such a life. 'What does eternity matter to me? To lose the touch of flowers and women's hands is the supreme separation,' he wrote in an essay on the Roman ruins of Djemila in Algeria. But he did not suggest a happy neo-paganism as a solution to all modern ills. He was aware of the despair of many people's existence in an age when belief in anything transcendent – a Christian (or any other) God, or the Marxist concept of History progressing towards a distant utopia – had vanished. Central to his outlook is the concept of the Absurd.

'Everything that exalts life adds at the same time to its Absurdity,' he wrote in *The Myth of Sisyphus*, his philosophical essay published in 1943. Camus accepted that life has no absolute, eternally grounded meaning to give our lives and actions significance. He calmly envisioned a future hundreds of thousands of years hence when humanity will have vanished from the face of the earth: Shakespeare, Michelangelo, the Pyramids and the Taj Mahal will all be erased or forgotten. This did not worry him for posthumous fame struck him as bogus. Faced with the revelation of humanity's cosmic insignificance, everyday actions or scenes, indeed all human efforts, suddenly appear absurd, totally devoid of meaning. Camus heroically rejected the easy option of nihilism – or suicide – accepting the absurdity of life in a world without a given meaning. Little wonder that he has been called (if half-ironically) a 'saint without a God'.

The Outsider

Camus' first successful novel, *The Outsider* was written in 1940 while he was living unhappily in Paris, longing to return to the sun of his native Algeria. (Algeria was then regarded as an integral part of France, not a colony.) Its hero Meursault is a young man working as a clerk. Tough and street-wise, much like Camus himself, Meursault is mainly notable for his failure to show any emotion. Seeing the body of his mother who has just died, he exhibits no grief but merely asks for a coffee and smokes a cigarette.

The next day, unperturbed, he goes swimming as usual before seducing a girl he knows at the office, Marie. When she suggests marriage, he agrees indifferently. Amused indifference is his normal reaction to life. Later, on the beach again with his friend Raymond and their respective girlfriends, he calmly watches Raymond beat up his own girlfriend before the two get involved in a fight with some Arabs. Soon after, Meursault again comes across one of the Arabs, who draws a knife on him. Stunned by the sun and heat, he shoots the Arab once, and then again four times, and is arrested by the police for murder.

Meursault is put on trial but, in a society as racist as French Algeria, a white man would not have been found guilty of murdering an Arab threatening him with a knife if he had expressed the smallest remorse. However, he tells the police that he feels only 'a certain vexation' about the murder. In court the prosecutor picks on his 'callousness' at his mother's funeral to show that he was 'already a criminal at heart', even 'morally guilty of his mother's death'. Not helped by a useless lawyer, Meursault is found guilty and condemned to death.

Meursault's crime is an *acte gratuit*, a gratuitous act, in the purest sense, but one for which he comes to takes responsibility. Sloughing off his earlier indifference, he accepts his destiny while continuing to live in an eternal present. Waiting in his cell he marks 'the summer evening coming on by a soft golden glow spreading across the sky'. At just that sublime moment the prison chaplain enters to offer his own banal brand of salvation and is angrily attacked by the condemned man for such impertinence.

Camus never intended Meursault to be taken as a role model for he is an incomplete man. If Meursault discovers his own integrity, it is as a figure from myth or legend. Sartre saw it as a 'novel about the absurd and against the absurd'. Iris Murdoch called *The Outsider* 'a compact, crystalline, self-contained myth about the human condition, as economical, as resonant as ... any piece of imaginative writing'.

The Plague

Camus wrote most of *The Plague* in 1941–2 while he was living in Algeria. He was actually teaching in Oran, the city in which the novel is set. However, the novel has no relevance to any recent epidemic in that port. What it reflects, if obliquely, is Camus' experience of the German occupation of metropolitan France and the resistance to it. He later returned to France to join the Resistance, editing *Combat*, the chief underground magazine.

The Plague is usually seen as a parable of France's occupation by the Germans, with those who volunteer to combat the plague representing the Resistance, the plague Nazism. Conor Cruise O'Brien called it 'a great allegorical sermon'. Some critics object that the reality of Nazism is ignored, the battle against an inhuman plague oversimplifying the problem of political commitment. However, *The Plague* is not a realistic but a symbolic tale. It makes no attempt to describe actual totalitarianism. Within the novel, it is the plague that deserves a star role, for it has long been seen as a symbol of evil beyond race, creed, sex or nationality. As Camus later commented, '*The Plague* can apply to any resistance to tyranny'.

The book won the Prix des Critiques on its publication in 1947 and became a bestseller. It is considered Camus' finest novel, among the greatest written during the Second World War, its understated tone far removed from the defiant hymn to solitude of *The Outsider*.

Postscript
Are existential questions still relevant?

In the 1960s, the dominant tradition in university departments in the UK and USA was linguistic. Philosophers explored the meaning of terms and showed their relationship to one another. Ethics was not about discussing right or wrong, but merely considering how one might justify and explain the nature of moral discourse. It was assumed that philosophers would *not* engage with the issues that confronted most people most of the time. Existentialism was something 'continental' and therefore, for many, off the radar.

Today the world of philosophy is very much broader. Philosophy, as an academic subject, maintains its intellectual rigour. But, to take Ethics as an example, the philosopher Peter Singer challenges moral assumptions about global issues and does not simply explore whether, and on what grounds, one might be able to make a moral statement. Outside the world of academe, philosophy has now returned partly to the streets, as it did with Sartre in 1945. There are philosophy cafés, where amateur philosophers meet to discuss topical issues, and popular magazines that may just as likely examine the philosophy of film or of science fiction, as feature articles on one of the great thinkers of the past.

And it is this engaged nature of recent philosophy that links it back to existentialism, since the most pressing issues today are existential. What should I do? What does it mean to be a human being? What values may I take as foundational? How do I affirm anything for myself in a relativist world?

In all this, there is a concern for personal meaning and significance — exactly what the existentialists were after in the heady years, when austerity was mixed with hope, after the Second World War. With hindsight, existentialism was a rebellion against a growing tendency to see science and overarching theoretical explanations as defining life. In their place, the existentialists wanted an awareness that was fully and practically embedded in life — a philosophy that would offer personal freedom.

So perhaps, far from seeing existentialism as a feature of a particular historical period, when the world, reeling from the chaos caused by two world wars, tried to reaffirm the value and significance of the individual, we should see an existential approach as the *norm*. From that perspective, the discussion of factual evidence and the analysis of linguistic form become important tools used by philosophy, rather than ends in themselves. It is the existential questions – Who am I? What should I do? – that should remain central to the task of philosophy.

So existentialism is far from over. It is now a feature of our everyday thinking, not a theory within the confines of academic philosophy. Discussion of marriage and the reasons for marriage breakdown now focus on the nature of personal satisfaction, or what someone is looking for in marriage, or the dangers of one or other partner becoming fixed in an inauthentic role from which he or she eventually, in order to 'discover their real life', feels the need to break free.

This language, influenced by psychology as much as philosophy, is profoundly existential; it is all about the experience of being a human being and relating to others. Unlike the field of neuroscience, which attempts to give an analysis of the working of the brain in order to explain our behaviour, thoughts and wishes, most therapies investigate the engaged human being. They look at involvements, commitments, desires, plans for the future, at the setting into which the human being has been thrown by circumstances and what he or she makes of it.

All that, as we can now recognize, is profoundly existential in its presuppositions. For life is there to be grappled with and affirmed, there to be lived authentically, free from the constraints that society is all too ready to impose. And that freedom, of course, was the central appeal of existentialism.